THE HORROR WRITER

A Study of Craft and Identity in the Horror Genre

Compiled & Edited by Joe Mynhardt

**A HellBound Books LLC
Publication**

www.hellboundbookspublishing.com

Printed in the United States of America

Contents

THE HORROR WRITER

A Study of Craft and Identity in the Horror Genre

Introduction

"What on earth makes you write such horrible things?"

As an author, don't you just hate that? For me, that particular question (if I'd had a dollar for every time I'd heard it... you know the deal) ranks all the way up there – along with *"Where do your ideas come from"* and *"Ooh, you really* must *write a novel about this awesome idea I have about a killer... (fill in your own blank here)."* For the writer – we architects of horror especially – dinner parties, kids' birthdays, and all manner of social gatherings can become quite the nightmare of Lovecraftian proportions.

Okay, we authors all know the what, and have a pretty good handle on the why, but what about the *how*?

And that, fellow writers of all things dark and terrifying, is precisely what we address in *The Horror Writer* – your definitive guide to the trials and tribulations of being a writer of this most insalubrious genre.

We have assembled some of the very best in the business from whom you can learn so much about the craft of horror writing: Bram Stoker Award© winners, bestselling authors, a President of the Horror Writers' Association, myriad contemporary horror authors of distinction with many, many years under their literary belts, and relative newcomers who have earned their horror writing chops just the same as everyone in the biz – the hard way.

The Horror Writer covers such critical issues as how to connect with your market and carve out a sustainable niche in the independent horror genre, how to tackle the writer's ever-lurking nemesis of productivity – just how *do* we increase that elusive word count? Naturally, it is as important to know how to write good horror stories with powerful, effective scenes, realistic, flowing dialogue and relatable characters as it is to be truly masterful in the art without resorting to clichéd jump scares and other all too well-worn gimmicks. Also covered is the delicate subject of handling rejection with good grace, and how to use those inevitable "not quite the right fit for us at this time" letters as an opportunity to hone your craft.

We have thrown into the pot a handful of decidedly perceptive interviews to give you an intimate peek into the psyche of the horror author and the challenges they work through to bring their nefarious ideas to the page.

And, as if that – and so much more – was not enough, we have for your delectation Ramsey Campbell's beautifully insightful analysis of the tales of HP Lovecraft. Enjoy a truly unique opportunity to learn from a modern grand master of horror as he dissects the works of a past master and one whose influence is ingrained in the very soul of practically everyone who is driven to write horror.

The Horror Writer is a wonderful, exciting departure for HellBound Books, insomuch it is our very first work of non-fiction. And, as such, this book is exclusively for you, dear writer, and those like you who aspire to chill blood and crunch bones with their words; it is most definitely *not* for the muggles who deem it acceptable to ask, "What on earth makes you write such terrible things?"

James H Longmore
HellBound Books Publishing LLC
January 2020

Connecting with Your Audience Through Fear

Chad Lutzke

Y ou're afraid of something.
Spiders, snakes, heights, graveyards, thunderstorms, tight spaces, being alone, basement stairs, dark hallways, the sight of blood. Every one of us has our individual fears. But what keeps you up at night may have zero effect on someone else. Another person may even revel in what you loathe. Thunderstorms being a good example. Some love the smell of rain, the sound of it as it taps the windows, the flash of lightning, the bruised clouds overhead bringing solace to one person and raising the blood pressure of another.

Clowns are another example. Personally, I've never found them even remotely scary; however, judging by the amount of films, Halloween costumes, and the last decade's popularity in the white-faced fiends, it's fair to say that many people find them disturbing.

There's a science behind this type of individuality, and it involves life experience.

A lot of our fears stem from childhood trauma, no matter the degree and whether we remember it or not. There is a negative somatic marker attached to an event, a place, a sound, smell, or sight. An instance that rubbed us the wrong way and left our subconscious with the message that this is something to be afraid of. Even an event as simple as visiting a circus, with our tiny, growing minds struggling to comprehend what could be so comically entertaining about a group of face-painted figures with red noses who refuse to speak, only glare behind unwavering eyes with painted smiles (or frowns). Your average young mind may struggle with the concept and deem the quiet, yet hyperactive, things as something dangerous and terrifyingly unpredictable.

As for me? I find them boring. I can't connect with that fear.

I'm currently reading Stephen King's *IT* for the first time, and while the image of the clown itself does no more for me than Mickey Mouse, I do connect with the fear itself, as well as the seemingly insignificant fears the children of Derry, Maine feel that year. Eddie's fear of getting sick, Ben's fear of being alone, their unifying fear of dying—at the hands of anything. The clown being nothing more than a face in a crowd of things that ends lives. A universal fear. So, it's not the clown itself that's scary for me, but the fear of death, the fear of a violent death. It's what connects me to those boys. Not my own fear of a clown, because there is none.

When I was a kid, my thing was fear of drowning. My mother tells me while taking swimming lessons as a child, the two instructors in charge were distracted with their flirting and petting while I struggled in the water, nearly drowning, until my mother saw and screamed for help.

Sounds like a familiar horror film plot, doesn't it? I should also mention the irony of me being born on Friday the 13th. Do with that what you will.

I didn't remember the incident, but my subconscious certainly did. And for a few years, I dreaded indoor pools. I still think they're creepy, but I eventually outgrew my fear of drowning, though for a while it was crippling. It was crippling because it was real. That fear didn't stem from urban legend, stories told of people being sucked under beds by boney-fingered hands, or rogue clowns tearing into the circus audience, abducting small children and eating them in front of their parents. Drowning can really happen. Drowning *does* happen.

When my father was young, he was inside a tiny fort made of cinder-blocks, when his brother sealed the thing and filled it with a nest of spiders. My father's body quickly covered in the eight-legged things while he sat screaming in total darkness, hundreds of legs skittering across his flesh. This made for a lifelong disdain for arachnids. While my wife, on the other hand, owned two tarantulas when I met her. She'd let them crawl all over her without a care in the world. That is until she developed an allergy over time that caused hives to form in her throat. And that was the end of that.

Through the years, as I developed a strong fascination with all things horror, it was never the fantastic that chilled me. It was the real-life scenarios, alongside some that were questionably believable, like hauntings and possessions.

But deep down, my biggest fears are the same as most: the fear of loss, be it losing one's mind, self-worth, life or that of a loved one. These are universally scary, and they are what I personally connect with most, which shows in my own writing. And because I write using my personal fears, the empathy is there, which in turn makes for a better connection with the reader. Essentially, I'm not faking it.

I also write with universal fear because I feel the topics connect with readers on a level deeper than say, a creature under a bed, a monster in the sea, or a brainless ghoul looking to add to their army of the undead. Don't get me wrong, the world needs stories like those. But to me, they're a different kind of ride. They're a fun scare. A safe one. You know full well no clown is under your bed, no blood-lusting vampire down the street in their dirt-filled coffin. But it's fun to pretend. It's fun to get a startle. But after you've read the last page and the book rests back on the shelf with its final pages filled with redemption, you feel safe. There were never any real zombies, no werewolves, no creatures of the night. Ghosts? Maybe. We're still not sure, though I think it'd be pretty cool. Demons? Another maybe, though I tend to believe there are. It's the real-life horrors that don't stay within that last page. They've long crept into your mind where they'll stay, given the story did what it set out to do. To make you think. To make you question. To make you uncomfortable because what you've just read about either *could* or *will* one day happen. Books with real-life horror force us to stare at the fear. They're less of an escape and more emotionally torturous, though subtle.

Most of Jack Ketchum's work does this. You think you're a badass until you read the horrifying things he's written for you. *The Girl Next Door* is on countless lists of people's most disturbing books they've ever read, one they'd never read again. One they sometimes wished they hadn't.

I never set out to deliberately damage minds, to leave the reader feeling hopeless. But there are life lessons to be found in legitimate fear, perspectives to be gained, blessings to be counted. Too many of us take our lives and loved ones for granted. Have you ever had a near-death experience? It changes you. I don't necessarily mean a permanent and drastic change in character—we're far too stubborn for that. I mean a different outlook. Whether you're living the experience yourself or investing in hours of reading about someone else going through it, you will still walk away learning something—a lesson from fictional experience without physically going through the turmoil yourself. Maybe when Ketchum wrote about that girl next door, he was doing the same. Scaring you into not being an asshole. Scaring you into giving a shit about people.

If a writer sets out to scare, it should come from experience, from a deep understanding of what it means to be afraid, whatever the fear. Fear in itself is just that. Your spider is my deep water. They cause the same reservation, the same racing heart. But I think the most convincing fear comes from those who offer up what actually scares them.

Why write what scares you? It's like telling a joke. We only tell the ones we think are funny. You'll never spread the word about a rabbi, a priest, and a monkey walking into a bar if you yourself don't find it worthy of a good laugh. It would make little sense for me to convince you to be afraid of clowns when I myself am not. Can it be done? Sure. But maybe not as successfully, the connection not as strong.

Now, this may sound like I'm preaching "write-what-you-know" advice, but I assure you I don't subscribe to that nonsense. That advice, if taken literally, is damning, and had past authors followed it there would be no Middle-Earth, no Frankenstein, no Derry, Maine. Yet, in a not so literal sense, we *do* write what we know. I know sadness. I know trauma. I know loss. I know violence. And each of them wears a mask. Stephen King's *IT* has one with a red nose. Jack Ketchum's has one with an emaciated, burned and beaten girl. So, in that sense—that you're already writing what you know—your personal experience can have a contagious effect on the reader.

At the risk of sounding like a hypocrite, scary isn't really what I go for when writing a story. I just want the reader to walk away from that closed book with a sinister smile on their face. The kind of smile you give when someone outsmarts you, when you can't help but respect them for their effort, offering a high-five at a job well done, and with a headful of far too much to think about.

But if scaring people is what you set out to do, write what scares you. The world is full of readers with your same fear that will connect even more. There are those who cover their eyes at clowns, refuse to dangle their feet over the end of the bed, cower at the twig-like legs poking from under a shiny, plump abdomen, or run up the stairs once the basement light is clicked off.

The empathy—that interconnecting and essential ingredient to any good story—begins with your own fear, having that intimate relationship with it. So, share the fear. You've been doing the research your whole life. Now share it. And in the safety of their favorite reading chair, someone's heart will race, their eyes will widen, the light will be left on, and the pages will turn. All because you wrote what you knew. You told the joke you think is funny, and now your laughter is infectious.

Focus!: How Writers Can Improve Their Productivity

Lisa Morton

Productivity—it's every writer's best friend or their arch-enemy, the master or the slave. These days, when there are hundreds of new writers popping up every year all vying for the attention of the same readers, controlling productivity is more important than ever. You need to capture your readership with great work, and then keep them interested by offering them a constant flow of new material. The days of lounging by the bottle of absinthe waiting for the muse to strike are long gone (if indeed they ever existed at all). Produce or die is the new mantra.

In other businesses, productivity might depend on management, on training, on equipment, or on wages and benefits. But we're writers; hopefully we don't have to deal with management often, we know that our training goes on perpetually, we already have the equipment (although see below for a note on that), and we laugh in the face of wages and benefits. In writing, productivity is probably most defined by two other factors: time and focus.

Anyone who has been writing for a while knows that the second most frequently posed question by non-writers (after the dreaded, "Where do you get your ideas?") is, "How do you find the time to write?" I have a standard response to this: "How much television do you watch?" This is usually met with a groan or an abashed nod, and the discussion is over.

But since you're reading this, you've already demonstrated that you have more than a casual interest in writing. You've already decided that writing (and reading this article) is more important to you than the television you could be watching instead right now, or the game you could be playing, or the messages on your phone you could be scrolling through, or the music you could be listening to. If someone asked you, "Why do you write?," your answer would be simply, "Because I have to."

But even with that dedication, time keeps slipping away from you. You've been working on the same short story for a month now, and somehow you can never seem to find the time to finish it.

Let's chat briefly first about your day job. Unless you're lucky enough to already be living the dream, you have a day job. I'm going to assume that you have a day job that doesn't leave you so overworked or stressed out that you're simply too exhausted to write. If you've got one of those jobs that requires you to work 70 or 80 hours a week, just stop reading this article right now. Seriously. You've already committed to one job to such an extent that you've left no time for a second one, and you need to think of writing as a full-time job in order to succeed. You're probably already late getting back to work anyway; go, be happy, make a zillion dollars, and leave the writing to those of us who are willing to work day jobs that allow us enough time and energy to write in our off hours.

So you're not watching the latest reality t.v. show, and you've got a nice, low-key job…but time still slips through your fingers faster than words do. This next part's gonna get ugly and is definitely not for the squeamish. Anyone who believes You Can Have it All should please leave the room now. Here's the tough love:

After that great time-sink that is television, the next biggest thing stealing your time is probably other people. Your friends want to go out. Your spouse wants to talk. Your kids want to play. All of them are taking time away from your writing, but their feelings will be hurt if you tell them that words on a screen are more important to you than they are.

Sorry, but you've gotta do it. Okay, maybe you don't have to phrase it exactly that way, but some lines must be drawn. Your friends and loved ones have to understand that you need their support to realize your goals, and that support may include telling them you can't go out to a club tonight or sit down on the couch to watch a movie. I've been a live-in caregiver to an elderly parent, and I occasionally hired a temp caregiver for no other reason than to give me a few hours to write. Telephones can be a big interference, and folks need to know that you may let yours roll over to voice mail or the answering machine if you're in the middle of writing. Make it clear to them that you consider writing a second job, and ask them if they'd barge into your office workplace just to gossip about who won *American Idol* last night or show you the new Lady Gaga video.

Even with self-discipline and understanding friends and loved ones, it's sometimes simply impossible to find hours at a time to write. That's why my last suggestion on managing your time is a little notion I've personally employed to great success for years:

Harness the power of the micro-session.

A micro-session could be as short as five or ten minutes, and is just what the name implies. I don't recommend micro-sessions as a complete alternative to real chunks of time set aside for writing—you can't really develop a plot or a character in just a few minutes. But micro-sessions work great for things like outlines, synopses, bios, queries, articles, or even those blog posts that'll keep your readers hooked.

Now, remember that mention I made at the beginning about equipment? Here's where I'm going to make that one suggestion: You need to find what works best for you, whether it's carrying a moleskin notebook and a pen, getting a dictating app for your phone, or figuring out some other way to put your phone to writing use. For me, I love to sprawl with a laptop, and the lighter and more portable the better. Yesterday I typed while I watched a friend's cat, while I took a break at the day job, and in bed just before I fell asleep. The equipment is enabling the micro-sessions.

Let's look at focus now. We've probably all had that nightmarish hour spent in front of a page or a screen staring at the same ten words typed yesterday, and feeling just completely hopeless. Most likely you're distracted, but you could also be simply indecisive. Perhaps you thought you knew where this story was going until you actually sat down to write it.

It all comes down to focus, and you don't have any.

I'm going to start by asking you a question: Have you ever worked on a writing piece with a deadline? If so, I'm betting you made the deadline, right? So, what was different between that project and your current piece, which is written entirely on spec?

The answer, of course, is obvious: the deadline. Somehow having a finish date pre-set for us and constantly looming seems to inspire that fickle muse to work harder and faster. The answer, then, is simple and usually surprisingly effective: Set deadlines for yourself. If you're working on more than one project, stagger the deadlines so you can finish one story before moving onto the next. Make the deadlines realistic (don't, in other words, aim at writing a novel in a week), and follow them. Understand that there will be a penalty to pay if you don't meet the deadline— you won't be able to start the next project on time. I have a whiteboard in my office that I write all of my deadlines on, positioned right where I can't miss it. Look at those deadlines every day; a little pressure is good for the writer's soul.

A few thoughts about word counts: some writers find it helpful to set themselves a minimum word count to meet every day. I once asked a successful mid-list writer about this (since that writer seemed extraordinarily prolific to me), and was surprised to hear that he aims for just 500 words a day. That doesn't seem like much on the surface— it's not even two complete double-spaced pages—but when you multiply it by 365 (and yes, this writer WILL work every day of the year), that means he's going to produce 182,500 words in a year, or two novels and some short fiction (and yes, I know I'm not counting rewrites). I have another friend who is frequently contracted to write movie and television novelizations on short schedules, and she knows she must sometimes manage at least 4,000 words a day. Personally, I don't set a minimum daily word count for myself; I may go days without typing a thing other than e-mails and Facebook updates, but during those days I might be researching or working out a plot in my head. Then, when I do sit down at last for a few hours, I may disgorge 10,000 words at once. The point is: If a daily word count requirement works for you, then find your optimum number and stick by it. If it doesn't, don't push it. You'll only make yourself unhappy, and unhappiness is a big distraction.

So are lots of other things. If you're having trouble seeing words materialize on that screen in front of you, take a look around and figure out why. Is it the work itself? Are you subconsciously telling yourself that something needs to be fixed in the work you've already done? I've noticed that writers seem to block most often at endings, and my advice is always this: If the ending isn't working, that means there's something wrong with the beginning. Read over what you've already done, and see if it jogs something loose for you.

Or is the distraction outside of the work? Granted, a lot of distractions you have no control over (I live right in the flight path of an airport, so I know all about unexpected big sounds), but others you do. Do you find your mouse cursor sliding over to that new game you just installed? Or are you just certain that you're missing the world's greatest Twitter trends while you try to pound out a few more words?

If you've already created a project schedule for yourself and you know how many words you want to achieve each day, then consider making the game or the social network part of your schedule, preferably as a reward. If you've set up your master plan to include writing from 6 to 9 p.m., then save your fun activities for after 9 p.m. If it helps, write this down on that list that's posted in your work area.

And don't forget to inspire yourself from time to time. What inspires you—a walk, a great song, a favorite movie? I tend to think of my own writing life as an input/output system—my output is much better when the input's been superior. Reading another writer's terrific story or seeing an amazing movie can pull me right out of writer's doldrums. In the midst of all that other scheduling mentioned above, I tried to leave a little time for the input part of the process, and experiencing something great invariably has me champing at my writer's bit.

I once heard a story about how the 19th-century British novelist Anthony Trollope worked (if you're not familiar with Trollope, all you need to know is that he's regarded as one of the most prolific writers of all time): Trollope wrote for exactly two hours every morning, and at the end of those two hours, he put down his pen, regardless of whether he was in the middle of a sentence or not, and walked away; the next morning, he started again, picking up exactly where he'd left off (he was also a postal worker who occasionally robbed the "dead letter" collection for inspiration). While I know I'm not capable of that—ahem—excessive compartmentalization, I applaud Mr. Trollope's work ethic and recognize the importance of creating my own schedule and methods of staying productive. Trollope, of course, didn't have the temptations of social networks and television to distract him...but somehow I'm guessing he would still have avoided those playthings of the Devil to stay focused and productive.

Remember: Those words aren't going to write themselves, and if you're going to be a career writer, productivity is what could make you—or break you.

An interview with Steve Rasnic Tem

Joe Mynhardt

Joe Mynhardt: What continues to draw you to the horror genre?

Steve Rasnic Tem: My goals in writing are quite similar to my goals in reading. I want to be moved. I want to feel something. I want writing capable of bringing me to tears. I want writing which reminds me of the things most important in my life. I want to be engaged in a real and authentic way.

And the older I get, my hunger only increases for those kinds of experiences. We're not here forever—why waste our time with the mediocre, the average, and the mundane?

There's nothing wrong with escape, of course. We all need to escape on a regular basis. Sometimes a good thriller novel will do that for me, or a particularly skilful action movie. Comedy is another form of escape, and I devour funny movies and plays and stand-up performances on a regular basis. I need at least one good belly laugh per day to maintain my sanity. But although some of my work contains thriller elements, and I've occasionally written a comedic story, those types of stories aren't my primary form of expression.

I think I was drawn to horror fiction initially because of its raw emotional quality. A major advantage of the genre is the elemental nature of fear. It's something everyone feels, and it's one of the strongest of our emotions. And the best horror stories also capably evoke what we love—that other powerful, overwhelming emotion. Because horror exists when who or what we love is threatened—our children, our lovers, our culture, our own lives.

The other aspect of horror which attracted me, and which still obsesses me, is the way it provides narratives about the unknown, the great mysteries, the invisible things which we do not understand and struggle for an adequate language to express. The "Weird fiction" label is often applied to this variety of horror, and although I'm not enthusiastic about labels I think it fits very well. One of the main reasons I started writing fiction was because I wanted to find a way to talk about all these invisible, mysterious things which felt as real and important to me as the realities I could see in my daily life. Horror fiction/weird fiction provided a methodology for that.

Joe: Tell us more about your mindset when you sit down to write. Do you mainly write to get the story out onto paper, to exercise and improve your craft, or with the purpose of publication?

Steve: My early writings were simple acts of self-expression. In an early essay ("Writing As a Way of Knowing") I said I often wasn't sure what I "knew" until I wrote it down, and I was always rather surprised by just how much I knew, the knowledge about human beings which came across on the page. I couldn't imagine where the knowledge came from.

I did write the occasional character sketch in the beginning, the exercise in descriptive writing, but I quickly grew bored with those kinds of exercises. I was interested in, obsessed with stories and what they could do, and I made it my mission to read as many examples of them as possible. And I started writing them even before I really understood what a story was, or at least what a "Steve Rasnic (later Tem)" story was.

Once I had some ideas about how to create stories, and became truly serious about my craft, I wrote stories with the intention of submitting them to editors and seeing them published. The stories were still about self-expression, they still met certain needs of mine to explore and discover, but the end goal was to see them in magazines or in books on bookshelves. So they had to be as good as I could make them, for wherever they might finally appear. It doesn't matter whether it's a big or a small market—readers judge you on the quality of the work in either case. That's pretty much my goal for all my writing—I write very little that isn't intended for eventual publication. Maybe not my rough notes or my personal letters and emails, but just about everything else.

I have no illusions I will be read in a few centuries time—at some level writers need to understand literary immortality is highly unlikely. But I think you need to write *as if* you're going to be read down through the ages. I don't know any other way to do it if you care about the quality of your work.

Joe: Do you have a special technique or guideline you follow to make your characters so real and three dimensional?

Steve: For me the key is to "inhabit" those characters as thoroughly as possible, especially the viewpoint character. In part you need to do what many actors do in preparing for a role. You need to hear the character's voice and thoughts in your head. Most importantly, you need to know what they care about most in the specific situation of this story. You need to thoroughly understand their attitude toward the unfolding events. I can't finish a story until I understand its emotional heart, and that heart comes from my viewpoint character. That's much more important than character description (in fact, I seldom describe my viewpoint characters in any great detail—I want to maximize reader participation, and encourage them to imagine the character in their own way). In my experience, when the prose and the dialogue is off, when the narrative voice isn't convincing, it's often because the writer hasn't adequately inhabited the viewpoint character. The answer is to revisit that character, or consider the possibility you need to choose a different character in order to tell the story properly. That's never welcome news—it often means a complete rewrite—but it may be necessary.

The goal of this inhabitation, or possession if you will, is to get to the point where the character can tell you what happens next, what is important, perhaps even what the story means. After all, it's *their* story. That doesn't mean you let them take over completely, but they have to have their say. Admittedly, some writers find that approach to be a bunch of mystical mumbo jumbo, but it's what works for me.

Another aspect to this is my belief a story is like a dream the viewpoint character has, and you can therefore apply the techniques of gestalt dream interpretation to its construction. In that theory every part of the dream—the setting, the events, the other characters—are actually projections and aspects of the dreamer—or in this case, the viewpoint character. I think this happens naturally—and unconsciously—as writers create stories; it's the glue that makes everything fit together. But it's something you can play with deliberately.

Joe: I'm sure a lot of the authors would like to know more about your preferred method of writing, and why. Do you just sit down to write or plot first? Do you write with pen and paper, typewriter or computer? In the privacy of your own home, outside or in a busy coffee shop?

Steve: Over the years I imagine I've tried every approach possible. At the very beginning I made copious handwritten notes about character, plot, dialogue, then came up with an outline to plug all of it into. I had to know both the beginning and the end and who most of the characters were before I began writing. I then typed all that up with a Hermes manual typewriter until I had a very rough draft. The draft was cut apart, rearranged, hand-written passages were taped into it, and there were scribblings everywhere. It was a real mess. I had to retype that manuscript over and over for numerous drafts and it took forever.

I did occasionally write stories out by hand in a notebook and later transcribed them. Sections of my novel *Blood Kin* were written that way. But for the most part I stuck with the typewriter until computers came along.

The advent of home computers opened up my process considerably. I was suddenly able to write things out of order, do an unlimited number of incremental drafts, etc. "Mind mapping" software gave me the ability to brainstorm electronically and to rearrange those ideas into a plot structure. This new-found freedom encouraged me to experiment with ways to increase productivity. I had several computers in different rooms in the house and I played with various mini-computers and hand-held devices so I could switch rooms and devices, including writing outside, depending on my mood or the story. If I got tired of working on one piece I'd switch rooms and work on something else in a different environment. It allowed me to work much longer and with less fatigue.

The switching of devices was not without its pitfalls. For example, my middle-grade novel *The Mask Shop of Doctor Blaack* was written on several different computers over the years, using a variety of operating systems and word processing software. At one point parts of it even existed on a tape drive for an old Commodore computer. I attempted to clean up the file when I transferred it to another computing environment of course—stripping it down to clean text and all that—but for some reason corruption continued to creep in. I have no idea why, but pulling together a final version was a headache both for myself and the copyeditor. The text appeared to be haunted by its previous versions.

I think all this experimentation freed up my process, and lead to the methods I use now. I normally use one desktop and one laptop, and everything goes into one text file. Most stories begin with a phrase or a bit of dialogue, and a vague notion of the theme I want to write about. I brainstorm directly in the file, typing up bits which sound like dialogue or someone's thoughts related to the theme. I also enter any research I've done on theme, character, setting. Eventually a character and an attitude emerges, and pieces of the plot. When I find the emotional heart—the narrator's essential relationship with the theme—the story really begins to take off, new events present themselves, and I go back to the beginning and edit, writing new bits related to my clarified understanding of the character, and deleting (or saving elsewhere) things which don't fit. By this time I usually know what the ending should be. Succeeding drafts are for refining things.

Joe: What advice do you want to give all the authors reading this book? Perhaps something you wish you'd done or learned early on in your career.

Steve: I think critical, "aware" reading is essential. If you want to write short stories, I suggest you read at least a thousand of them representing all genres and styles critically. How did the writer begin the story? How did he or she end it? Make a list of the beginnings and endings you particularly like. If you do this conscientiously you will develop an inventory of possible beginning and ending strategies for your tales. It's an area that can be especially troublesome for inexperienced writers. Do the same for "middle" strategies. How did the author get from point A to point B? How did the author keep you reading? Was there some sort of structure involved? Rising and falling action? Subplots? Complications? Just pondering these issues in specific examples can teach you a great deal about writing.

Jump-scares: Creating Tension Without Gimmicks

Kenneth W. Cain

All of us have seen an atypical jump-scare in a movie. For instance, a young man or woman walking down a dark corridor with many intersecting hallways, fearful some monster will jump out and hurt them. The big screen and little screen have an advantage over writing when it comes to jump-scares. There's the way they shoot the scene, the accompanying music that builds and rises in volume as we reach that moment. And it's become as popular in recent movies as ever, so it makes sense writers would try to incorporate them in their fiction. Only, the formula isn't quite the same for writing horror.

As writers, we don't have the advantage of adding a soundtrack to everything that happens in our stories, so we don't exactly use jump-scares, not in the form most viewers would recognize them. When we do, we often rely on words like "suddenly" to achieve this effect, albeit insufficiently. Very few readers, if any, will read the word "suddenly" followed by some intense moment in our story and react as we would hope. Therefore, using adverbs like this to express urgency won't work the same for our stories as they do in our heads. We can achieve a similar feel, though more goes into scenes like this than adding a few convenient words. Writers have to build up to that moment, unlike our film-based colleagues, though it's not altogether different. Creating tension in writing requires atmosphere and character building. Look at any visual sequence and you'll find those elements are there too, just maybe not so in-depth in perception.

The first ingredient in building tension is character traits. Focusing on our example, what type of person do we have walking down this hallway? Are they an overly confident sort of person? Or are they more the terrified kind? Their personality will help determine their reactions. It matters who your characters are because it establishes how they respond to whatever tension we apply to any situation. A confident character might not react at all to a noise, while a terrified character might take off running the second they hear anything out of the ordinary. Sometimes, the latter variety are the most fun characters to play with in your writing sandbox.

As you likely know, there's a lot more that goes into character building than just that. To make your characters feel real to a reader, you must build their personality, create likable and relatable characters that the reader can connect with. To achieve this, ground your characters in the real world, even if that world is made-up. More so, every detail you slap onto their build also affects how they react to certain stimuli. Even the clothes they wear will help define their personality, though you don't want to list these details in order. Reveal qualities of your characters as they move through their world. And, as they move about and interact with other characters and objects, endure the standard trials and tribulations of life, their character evolves. A strong character might devolve into the complete opposite and vice versa, further complicating matters. Or, they might not change at all, depending on how determined and hardheaded of a character we are depicting.

Let's say you have a rebellious male character. Maybe he snagged his shirt on some barbed-wire, jumping the fence to check out an old abandoned hospital. How would that change him? How could that affect what happens next? That might depend on many factors. What kind of shirt is it? Is it from a special concert, maybe the last one he attended with a very close friend before that friend died? What sort of band defines this rebel? Is it his favorite band? And his reaction to this rip can also help to further define his character. Does he throw a fit? Give up? Or does it push him onward, more determined than ever to finish the task?

Speaking of building character, each one should be unique. This can be one of the more difficult tasks for some writers, as you want to avoid having your characters appear like cookie cutter copies of one another. You want to prevent creating two-dimensional characters, and instead focus on developing fully rounded, deep thinking, unique characters. Each should have their own opinions, their own feelings, their own issues and obstacles, hurdles they must jump to help define who they will become. Once again, it's important not to info-dump these details into your story. Seed these specifics throughout the narrative as the character interacts with this world you've created, which brings us to the next component.

Setting can also have a large impact on creating good tension. You can seed elements of the setting throughout your prose, so that when our terrifying moment comes, it's shocking not only to the reader but to our character. Is the fence rusted? What does the hospital look like? Is he afraid? It's cliché, but, for our example, does lightning strike in the background? Is it nighttime? What's the weather like? These factors help define your character's responses as things happen to them and help to build your character's personality. You're the creator here, taking a skeleton and slapping on some muscle, veins, flesh, skin tone. This is how you make your characters feel like they're grounded in the real world, but adding some real-world objects into the mix can further that along. But be careful not to deprecate those entities. Or you can use objects in more of a general sense and achieve the same goal.

In our example, our rebellious character has just jumped over the rusted fence and torn his shirt (a vintage Twisted Sister concert T-shirt). He's approaching a dark building at night, thinking of his dead friend and the shirt with not a single light to guide him but the glow of the moon. Maybe he forgot his flashlight, so he's forced to use an app on his cellphone when he gets to the hospital. We've created some atmosphere and we haven't even entered the building yet. Now we've introduced this new complication, which reduces our bold character to more of a downtrodden person because of what just happened. Forced to rely on this technology, that's when he realized the battery is low. Here, we're creating tension we will capitalize on later in the story.

Our character gets to the door and finds the lock busted. The door hangs loosely in its frame, so it's easy to open. When he yanks the door open, it's an opportunity to hit on some other senses, right? This is all part of building the setting and character and most of all, tension. What does he feel? Does an unnatural warm air rush out? What does it smell like? Is there a musty odor, or is it something metallic and gross? What is our character's reaction to this? For our purposes, let's say the air is cold and smells of something coppery like blood, an instant threat to our character, but despite not feeling so great about the shirt and his lost friend, our character still has that rebellious nature, so he's determined to get inside. And this begs another question.

What's his reasoning for being there? Is it solely because of his inquisitive nature, wanting to explore an apparently haunted facility? Or is it something more complex? Creating a need helps solidify the character in the scene. If he has a want, then he'll be in it to win it, and he'll keep going as long as he believes he's safe. Maybe one of his friends dared him to bring back some object from inside. What kind of hospital is this? What unique object could be our quest item for this scene? Giving your character's goals helps keep them vested in the task. This also creates more tension. For our example, let's say our character needs to secure an old scalpel or the like to gain the praise of his peers. He's determined, so little will persuade him to abandon the undertaking.

However, we can break even the boldest of characters. Part of the fun of writing is having that power, the ability to take a very confident, strong character and break them. But, like Tobey Maguire's Spider-Man, "with great power comes great responsibility." We have an obligation to make our fiction seem as real as possible. If we create a rebellious character and have them freak out over the smallest misstep, we will not have done well with staying true to their character. He's a rebel, and he will not be afraid of just anything. Nor will he freak out over just anything. Though this character has vulnerabilities, he's more resilient than the average character. He isn't brave so much as his experiences have worn him down. He's seen bad things that have changed him forever, such as his friend dying. This character is willing to accept that there are strange forces out there in the world, but he's perfectly fine with facing his fears to achieve a goal. Our responsibility as a writer is to stay true to this character's traits.

So, our character is walking down this darkened corridor, having just entered the building, and now we can capitalize on some of that groundwork we've laid out. The door slams shut behind him. This would startle most everyone, but when our character turns around, instead of seeing some monster, all he sees is that the door blew shut because of the wind. He hears another noise, slight, but there all the same, coming from somewhere deeper in the facility, he thinks. It doesn't alarm him, not yet, but he's definitely curious what that sound is and what made it. Still, our character ventures along the corridor, checking behind him once or twice, just to make sure nothing is following him because the door slamming shut unnerved him.

It isn't until we get out of reach of the door that the light emanating from his phone goes dark. Here's where we have to stay true to our character. He's not the sort to panic. All the same, it's not a situation even the most strong-willed character would handle well. There's some level of concern, and he wants to hurry and get what he came for and get the heck out, so he wants to reestablish the light as soon as possible so he can see to ease any concerns. That's when he sees the screen and realizes his thumb must have accidently turned the light off. But he also has this weird feeling that something is here with him, which makes his urgency for regaining that light even more pressing. As the tension builds, so does the possibility some stranger could be with him here in the dark, so his need to see continues to flourish, feeding his fears, weakening his resolve. Despite a couple missed attempts, he gets the light back on and what does he see but...

Nothing.

This is your jump-scare. But be careful because it can be

gimmicky. Overusing any technique in writing can devalue the instances where you really want the impact. It isn't about having ten to twenty jump-scares packed into a single scene. It's about creating tension and maintaining that tension throughout the scene. And not every scene requires tension. As we've already explored, build your characters and your scenery and your conflict, the arc of the story. You're working your way up to these scenes, hoping to establish a certain impact that will further cement the reader's connection to your story. We want fully vested readers interested in the story's outcome.

As our character moves down the hallway, he encounters obstacles in the form of intersecting hallways and doorways. With each new opening, the tension builds because our reader is expecting something to leap out and attack our character. And as our character nears and passes each, that tension flexes. There's a moment of ease followed by the reoccurring building of tension. It's like waves of dread, hitting our reader, assaulting their senses. That's what we're hoping to accomplish, all in building this scene, seeing our character get closer to their end goal while experiencing all this atmospheric tension. But, for our example, these intersecting hallways and rooms are mainly just a smokescreen, the possibility of a jump-scare being what the reader expects, thus bringing them deeper into our world.

One room has just what our character needs. They see this and enter, fully expecting to get what they came for and get the heck out, fast. See, not only have we taken our reader along for the ride, but we've created tension that has changed our character to a degree. Sure, he entered the building feeling rather strong, but his will has been breaking, little by little. He's weakened. There are cracks in his defenses that are widening and deepening. We're tearing him down and playing upon these newfound weaknesses, thus creating more tension. And now that we're finally here, right where he needs to be, there's a sense of accomplishment. Everyone is breathing a sigh of relief, because our character has made it to the end and will get what he came for without a hitch. Only, we're not quite done.

When our character sees the scalpel and moves to retrieve it, his phone dies. We need to touch on all the rational ideas here. Our character checks to make sure his thumb didn't accidently close the app again. Is it powered on? Of course, it is. Maybe banging it against his palm will jar something loose. Remember, he's reached a point of desperation here. He needs that light because it's all he has right now. Without it, he's in complete darkness. When he can't get the light back on, he experiences panic on a whole other level. It doesn't matter how bold he is anymore, because heck, he's in what appears to be a haunted hospital in complete darkness all by himself. But our character, being so rebellious and wanting to fit in, will not surrender. He wants that dang scalpel.

He lets his trembling fingers explore the table, searching for the object by touch. What other items might he feel? Does he know what each object is? Or, are some unknown? Are some items otherworldly, or are they familiar but unexpected? What if he feels something slimy on the table? Here's another opportunity to build tension, right before we reach the final objective. Even once he has the object he came for, the battle isn't over. Our character still needs to get out of the hospital alive and with that object in his possession, which might be easier said than done. It's up to you how far this goes, and remember, too much of a good thing can have an adverse effect on the reader. This is where you as a writer determine whether or not our character will succeed, whether he lives or dies or only gets hurt. Much of this depends on the overall story arc, but for our instance, our character finds the scalpel and takes off running in the dark.

Trying to remember the way out, our character encounters some trouble. He bangs into a table, into a doorway, and once he's in the hall, he can't recall which way is which. Before he can figure this out, he hears that strange noise, and this time it sounds so much closer. In fact, when he hears it again, he swears it's coming from directly behind him. What else is in this room? Did something come to life? Is it a ghost? Now our character is breaking. Panic is rising, tension rising, he has his quest object and needs to escape, but he's worried he might not make it. Adrenaline is rushing. Perhaps he accidently cuts himself with the scalpel. Blood flowing faster as he continues to run in the following scenes.

He takes off jogging in the direction he believes will lead to the exit. On the way, he's staggering about, bouncing off walls and running into doorways and such. There's a real struggle to escape. Behind him, whatever made that noise is chasing him. He can hear it dragging something along the floor. What can it be? This multiplies his sense of urgency. Our character is rifling through ideas, trying to think of how to get out, all the while searching for the way. And it isn't until he's gone too far that he finally realizes he's gone the wrong way. Now, because he only knows of the one way out, he either has to find another escape or go back the way he came and face whatever is chasing him. And whatever is following him is already here, making that strange noise, a sort of grunting whimper. The smell is intense, musty yet unlike anything he has smelled in his entire life. And this…

Is where we'll stop our example.

My goal here was to help you understand that using a word like "suddenly" isn't creating tension. That word isn't making a reader jump out of their chair either. As writers, we have a responsibility to make scenes feel as real as possible. Hopefully, I've helped you see how to create tension and maintain it, not only through situation but through character building and establishing scenery. Hitting on all the senses will help ground the scene in reality, and tying those elements to your character and scenery helps make it all feel complete.

Next time you're contemplating adding a scene like this, consult your personal history. Think of a time when the lights went out during a thunderstorm or something similar, whatever real-life situation you've encountered that best fits with your planned scene. How did you react? What did you feel? What smells and sounds stood out to you? Right there you have the basic elements for creating effective tension without relying on convenient words that do little to further your story.

Five years in the Horror Market

Kevin J. Kennedy

I became a writer accidentally. I never had any aspiration to be a writer, but I was always an avid reader. My taste has always been mainly horror, but I did read a lot of biographies and Irvine Welsh books. That being said, ninety-five percent of what I read was horror.

Due to this fact, I was on a lot of Facebook pages for horror authors, publishers, and book reviews. I always liked seeing what was coming out next or what authors I love were reading and recommended. I've been following my favourite authors from back in the days of poor websites and clunky message boards.

The first message board I ever came across was Richard Laymon's official one, that was linked to his site. I think I found it just months after he'd died, but it was also round about the same time that I had just finished reading everything he had written. I had tried several other horror authors that I found in the UK Borders stores such as James

Herbert, Dean Koontz, Stephen King and Anne Rice. I didn't enjoy any of them near as much as I did Laymon. I did fall in love with Anne Rice's Vampire Chronicles and that kept me busy for a bit, but I didn't enjoy any of her other work. I bought countless books that I couldn't finish because they were long and drawn out and didn't have Laymon's flare for keeping a story fast-paced and exciting. I guess what I'm trying to say is that I much preferred pulp horror to literary horror and it wasn't available to me in UK book stores. As the years passed there have been various new sub-genres that have appeared, but I consider Laymon a pulp writer and that's exactly what I enjoy.

Back in 2001 to 2003, the market had dried up to new horror in my opinion and publishers were printing anything that big names put out, even if it was terrible. I believe fans of the genre were looking for something new. Mass market releases have more misses than hits, if you ask me. I feel they push writers to go for the long, drawn-out tense kind of horror and it's just not my scene. I've also heard a lot of writers say they had to change parts of their books they didn't want to. That didn't work for me.

Enter the days of finding the Laymon message board and within a day of posting my tastes, I had about 80 messages from people with similar taste in horror, letting me know of either authors or books they loved, and being honest, I had never heard of most of them. After doing some research on the early Amazon site, I found four books that had been recommended that were right up my alley. The four books that I chose from the list, primarily because they came up so often, were: Ray Garton's *Live Girls*, Edward Lee's *City Infernal*, Jack Ketchum's *Off Season* and Brian Keene's *The Rising*. After reading so many books that I didn't enjoy or that I gave up on half way, finding these four books—and reading them back to back— made me realise there was so much great horror out there.

However, it wasn't coming from the big publishers and it wasn't being widely promoted. I had to look deeper for the stuff I wanted.

Jump to 2014 and I read almost entirely mid-market to indie horror, with my few dips into mass market stuff ending in massive disappointment. This is probably why I was on so many book review sites, blogs, Facebook pages and multiple other sources of horror info. The guys writing this stuff and publishing it neither had the money nor the power to shove it in your face the way the big four do.

Back then I was probably reading around eighty horror novels a year and maybe five of those were mass market at a push. I had gone through a rough time in my life and was at a stage where I was just endlessly scrolling through Facebook on my phone, and only really stopping at posts that had a picture of something horror related. I came across an advert for a book that was taking short story submissions. It was an anthology called *Fifty Shades of Slay* by Alucard Press. I liked the title. I'm a big fan of the cheesiness that horror sometimes brings, and this title made me laugh. I wrote my first ever short story, not because I wanted to be a writer, but because I needed a distraction. I expected an email back thanking me for sending it in but telling me it wasn't up to scratch. A little while later I got an email accepting the sub and telling me the editor was hoping to have two stories by each author in the book. I emailed back telling them I wasn't an author and wasn't sure I had a second story in me, but they asked if I would consider it and send them something to have a look at. I wrote a second story and subbed that, too. A few weeks later I had a bit of a bug in the back of my brain that said I should find another open call and send something in to see if I could get something else picked up. I liked the idea of a story of mine appearing in a book and, while I didn't expect much more than that, I felt I may in time, get a few shorts in a few books.

I spent the next year googling 'open calls to horror anthologies' and similar searches and sending in short stories to whatever ones I fancied. I was relatively successful and got quite a few shorts picked up. I guess like most writers I then watched these books to see how they performed.

The first thing that I noticed was that some publishers I had stories accepted to sold almost no copies of the books. If I'm being honest, I'm not surprised. Some of the covers looked like they had been drawn by a 4-year-old and the publishers didn't market the books from what I could see. The copies sold were almost guaranteed to have been bought by the authors and probably their friends and family. Although I had never wanted to be a writer, this didn't sit well with me. If I did sit down and write a story, I wanted to know what others thought of it. On reflection, my early work wasn't great. I'm sure if there were more reviews, my stories wouldn't have had much praise, but at the same time, I could have used the feedback. After about a year of doing this, I realised it wasn't for me. The novelty of having a story in a book had worn off. It was definitely an achievement, but I no longer got any joy from it. At this point, it would have been easy to just quit and live with the idea that I had a few stories in a few books and move on with other stuff. As I said, it was never an ambition of mine to be an author, so I would lose nothing.

Jump to a few months later: I had stopped looking at open calls and went back to reading. I still watched the market—something I had always done as I was always looking out for my next great read—but now I had started to watch certain indie and mid-market publishers. I was watching how they operated and what they were putting out, and a few clicked with what I was looking for. After some serious consideration, I decided to put my own anthology together. I knew it could be a disaster, but I had a feeling that if I got enough stories that I enjoyed, it would also have to be a decent book for others to read. I was just unsure of how many good stories I would get as I was not a publisher and had never done anything like this before. By this point I was following a load of indie writers and had read books by them all, so I knew whose stories I liked and whose style of writing I enjoyed. I sent an invite to maybe fifteen authors and was blown away by the fact that at least twelve of them said they would send me something. I wasn't sure much would come from it, but I kept my fingers crossed.

As I said earlier, I had been following the horror market for a long time by now and the one thing that always annoyed me was the lack of decent Christmas horror. Simply because of that, the first anthology I was going to put together was one of Christmas horror. Since I couldn't find what I was looking for, I decided to put one together myself. I felt that filling a gap in the market would surely get some interest, but it was still a gamble. Maybe no one did Christmas horror because no one wanted to read it. Either way, I was in and had planned to put a decent book out for readers. At that point I had no idea about covers or editors, but I knew I wanted solid stories to put together.

When the stories started coming in, I was a bit taken aback by the quality and suddenly realised that I was putting a book together whether I knew what I was doing or not. I managed to get Lisa Vasquez involved, from Stitched Smile Publications, and she came up with a stunning cover for me. I then got a recommended editor involved, Brandy Yassa, who is still working with me to this day.

I decided to contact some of the authors I had been reading over the last twenty years to see if they would be interested in taking part. I assumed that I would get almost no responses or some nice rejection letters, but also felt I had nothing to lose. A few of the authors I had followed for close to two decades sent me a story. This just felt mental, but also gave me the confidence to push on. I felt there must have been something in what I was doing to get these guys involved. I was right. The Christmas book hit the top of the charts in the US and UK upon release, and stayed there for quite some time, long after Christmas had passed. It continued to sell throughout the year which I found amazing as it was a Christmas book, but it gave me some confidence that I understood the market and what readers wanted.

For the next two years I still wrote short stories and submitted them to publishers, but I became more careful about who I sent my work to. I feel I took more time on the stories and rewrote them several times and even gave up on ones that I just didn't feel were strong enough. In the early days, I think I just subbed everything in the hope it would end up somewhere. These two things probably were a major reason that I ended up in some anthologies that weren't great, but I feel it's worth newer authors knowing this. The buzz will eventually pass and when you look back, you don't want to have lots of subpar work out there. I'm sure not everyone is in the same boat as me but, as I say, there is that buzz you get from having your story picked up. It can become addictive, then there is a little bit of a drive to sub to everything. It doesn't mean it's a good story just because someone is going to put it into print and that is what I had to learn. Validation means nothing from a crap publisher.

As time moves on, if you are keeping busy and writing a lot you will find you can't sub to everything and will become more selective anyway. Nevertheless, if this saves you from subbing to the wrong types of publishers, I'll feel pretty good about that. Some of the crap that comes out is the reason so many people avoid the indie market, but at the same time, I get the need to have your work out there. Just realise, that if your work is being rejected by decent publishers, there is probably a valid reason for it.

A lot of publishers won't touch your work if you don't already have a few pieces out there. I understand the reasoning behind this. They want authors in their books that already have a following as it's basically free marketing for them. If you get an author who already has an email list, often thousands of followers, they are going to send an email to all of them, telling them that they are in a new anthology and surely some of them will buy it. That being said, I find that new and upcoming indie authors are much more likely to share the book multiple times than more established writers, so it can go either way. You may feel I have moved away from the author life and started talking about anthologies quite a bit, but I know very few authors who don't feel that this is a great way to get exposure when you enter the market. Just be choosy and do your research.

Exposure is probably another point we should touch upon. I read posts on Facebook every day where people talk about the indie market and anthologies. Some authors don't do anthologies, they just release novels. Some managed to have their first book picked up by a reasonably sized publisher who will do a bit of marketing for them. I completely understand why this is a win. You get good exposure, a few quid in your pocket and probably a fair amount of reviews.

Some mass market books are exceptional, but some are just another version of the same old story. I find if you go through the indie market you find more original material and also some new styles. Their books haven't been battered to death by an editor who's never written anything. What I have come across is some bitterness from mass market authors. Being in the antho market, I often contact authors that I've enjoyed a book or two by and offer them a slot in one of my anthologies. Sometimes you get an author you have been a fan of for a long time working with you, sometimes you get a rejection because the author is too busy with current projects and sometimes you get a lecture because of what you are trying to do.

One author who I love gave me a two-hour lecture on why I shouldn't price Kindle books at 99p/$1.28 and told me the reviews on my books didn't count because anyone would give a 99p book a decent rating. I don't agree with that. I've given free books a low rating because I felt they wasted my time. Everyone has their own opinion. Also, the mass market author who gave me a hard time dropped the price of all their Kindle books to 99P three months later for quite some time, so I suppose the lesson here is don't listen to everything you are told as some authors are just trying to keep as much of the market as they can for themselves. Consider who is telling you what and look at where they are. Is it good advice or are they self-serving? It's the same as when the big four post their crap about the Kindle market dying off or it's just a fad. Never heard so much shit in all my days.

The other thing you will likely be told if you join the writing game is that you shouldn't give your books away for free. FUCK THAT!!! It's your book. If you want to do a free giveaway, do it! I find that my book sales spike after a giveaway and it gets you reviews which in turn get more sales. The person telling you this often has someone marketing them. I can't quite see how being indie and giving away some books is any different than someone paying to say their books are great in a magazine or wherever they advertise, but, as I said earlier, everyone has their own opinion. Just think about if the advice they are giving is to benefit you or them. The amount of people writing horror now compared to twenty years ago is incredible. That creates some competition. How do you get in front? Get your books to as many people as possible. How do you do that? Freebie! It doesn't make your book worthless. It just quickly gets it into the hands of lots of people. If they review it and if the reviews are positive, you will then get more sales. If the reviews aren't great, that's down to you. You need to write something else.

I will give another example of why I think writing something and giving it away for free is a good idea. I pay authors for stories to every anthology I have published, apart from my very first—at that point I had no money and no idea if it would sell. Since it did well, I've since paid for every story I have published, apart from the drabbles in the 100 Word Horrors books. These books contain 100-word stories; book 1 had 110 stories and book 2 had over 120. I could not afford to pay the authors for that volume of stories, but it was a book I wanted to do. No one had to sub, no one had to get involved, and no one had to read it. I just wanted to do it. There are now two books in the series with a third in the works and they are incredibly popular.

Now, you could decide that giving away your work for free is not for you, but I would argue that being in a popular book allows new readers to find you. Just read the reviews; loads of people say they found new authors they will try. If I had listened to the mass market guys and the folks who gave me shit, I would probably never have had anything in print and, if I'm honest, I'm doing better than I ever imagined by doing things my way. You must look at the market you are in. Some people will give you advice on something they know nothing about.

From what I've seen, most people don't start out by writing a novel. Some may, but I think a lot of people seem to start out with short fiction and move on. Since it's been my experience in working with a high number of short story writers and am familiar with what they go through, that's all I can really talk about.

What I will say is that I think everyone should take their own path. Don't listen to me and don't listen to the mass market guys who are worried about their sales dropping due to the indie market getting bigger. I've listened for years to people saying Kindle would die off and paperback would be king again. It's bullshit. I love Kindle and so do a massive amount of people. Why would it go away? It's convenient. I barely even use any of my Kindles anymore, but I always have a Kindle app on my laptop and phone, and it means I can read anywhere. I rarely carry an actual book with me. 99p and free books mean readers get to try new authors.

If you release your own Kindle book, you can give it away for free for 5 days out of each quarter. What better way is there to get your work in front of loads of people without spending a fortune on advertising? Getting your short into an anthology that thousands of people read…is that better than a small payment or are you in it for the cash? What I would say in this instance is, we all want the cash but if your early book isn't selling, how do you become a more recognizable name? People will lead you in a direction that benefits them. I, on the other hand, would rather have a book full of unheard-of authors that sent me great stories than a book of big names that put out whatever they could be bothered with because anything they write gets accepted. I'm confident that my views will bring back some negativity. I'm sure I know who it will come from, but I don't really give a fuck. Ask anyone who's ever worked with me. I'm honest and I help those who ask for my help, when I can. I'll always be around. Writing is a part of me now and the horror world was always a part of me. I'll die doing this shit and I'm sure I'll piss off some people along the way. Doesn't change anything. My work's out there and being enjoyed by a lot of people. I'm sure it was Laymon who said in *A Writer's Tale*, "Just keep writing." Simple but true. If you want to be a writer, stop fucking about on Facebook. Write something, then write something else. You'll get stronger with every story you write.

King of the Hill
Stepping out of the Shadows

Monique Snyman

L iving in an age where big-name authors like Stephen King, Clive Barker, Peter Straub, and Neil Gaiman often dominate the field, it is somewhat understandable to want to be exactly like them. To achieve the same success as the abovementioned authors is, for many, the ultimate goal of writing. What is often forgotten, however, is that there will always be just one Stephen King, one Clive Barker, one Peter Straub, and one Neil Gaiman. It is due to this inherent need to be as great as [enter influential author's name] that most writers have, at one point or another, struggled to carve out an identity for themselves in the horror genre.

Who they want to be often contradicts who they are, thus a crisis develops.

This crisis may not be easily averted for some, seeing as every writer is influenced by other authors' works. Whether it is the setting in a book that inspires, a particular character that prickles the imagination, or a theme an author wishes to further explore, both direct and indirect influences are unavoidable. One's writing style—the literary fingerprints of every writer—is much more difficult to copy, and any attempt to do so will probably not go down well in the industry. Nevertheless, no matter how saturated the industry seems to have become, it is possible to carve out a place for yourself without needing to resort to copycat writing.

Case and point: Joe Hill.

Most of the horror community now knows that Joe Hill (Joseph Hillstrom King) is the son of writers, Stephen King and Tabitha King, but this knowledge wasn't always readily available. Back in 1997, Hill chose to use an abbreviated form of his given name in order to see if he could achieve independent success based on his own merits, rather than as the son of an author whose name is synonymous with "horror."

It was a risky move, but in 1999, Hill received the A. E. Coppard Long Fiction Prize for "Better Than Home." In 2005, Hill's first book, the limited edition collection *20th Century Ghosts*, won the Bram Stoker Award for Best Fiction Collection, together with the British Fantasy Award for Best Collection and Best Short Story for "Best New Horror." It was only then that online speculation began as to who Joe Hill really was.

In 2006, *Vanity Fair* broke Joe Hill's cover in an article, and in 2007—a decade after Hill's first professional sale—he finally publically confirmed his identity.

At that point, however, Hill had already sold his first novel, *Heart-Shaped Box* to William Morrow, which was due to be released. *Heart-Shaped Box* reached number eight on the New York Times bestseller's list. *Locke & Key*, a comic book series published by IDW Publishing, released in 2008, and sold out of its initial print run on the first day. Filming for an adaption of *Locke & Key* by Netflix started in 2019. By 2010, Hill's second novel, *Horns*, came out, and a film starring Daniel Radcliff released in 2014. Hill's third novel, *NOS4A2*, was published in 2013, and peaked at number five on the New York Times' bestseller's list. A 10-episode television series was adapted from the novel by AMC, starring Zachary Quinto, and premiered in 2019. Hill's fourth novel, *The Fireman*, came out in 2016 and hit the number one spot on the New York Times' bestseller's list. In 2018, a collection of four short novellas titled *Strange Weather* was published.

Most, if not all, of the horror community doesn't doubt Joe Hill's ability as a great horror author. His writing style, although somewhat similar to Stephen King, is not a watered down version. Comparisons can be made between Hill and King, there are also instances of crossovers (*NOS4A2*, for example, sets Christmasland within Stephen King's Dark Tower universe), but one thing is certain: Joe Hill has his own identity in horror without having become Stephen King 2.0.

Another author who can be called a "legacy writer" is Christopher Rice, son of renowned horror novelist Anne Rice and poet Stan Rice. Unlike Joe Hill, Rice never hid his identity from anyone, but he still achieved success without relying on his name alone. His first novel was released in 1999, *A Density of Souls*, and was highly successful in both the gay community and with mainstream audiences. The novel also became a New York Times bestseller. Although Christopher Rice distinguished himself early on in his career by saying he wrote thrillers instead of horrors like his mother, Rice has dabbled in the genre, too. His works, *The Heavens Rise* and *The Vines*, were both nominated for the Bram Stoker Award in the Superior Achievement in a Novel category, but unfortunately lost out in the last round.

Christopher Rice, often viewed as being a multi-genre writer, has a firm grip on his identity as both a person and as a writer. Thus, even if—as it was recently announced—Rice collaborates with his mother on a project, there will be a clear distinction between styles, because they each have their own personality and it shows on paper.

It is incredibly important to understand that it's perfectly fine to want to be as great as your favorite author, but you need to be you regardless of how tempting it is to just copy and paste a well-known's life over your own. Besides, wouldn't you rather be seen as the first [enter your name here], and see your name alongside the greats', instead of being known as another wannabe [enter an influential author's name here]?

Take, for example, *Stranger Things*. The Duffer Brothers—Matt and Ross Duffer—are the creators of the hit Netflix series, but it only came into existence after they wanted to adapt Stephen King's *It* and Warner Bros. weren't interested. So, what did the Duffer Brothers do? They created something completely different, whilst showing homage to Stephen King, Steven Spielberg, and John Carpenter. Influence is everywhere, homage is a nice little Easter egg for fans if you share a demographic with one of the authors who've influenced your career, but beware! If you cross the invisible line, you may be heading into plagiarism territory, and it is not a place *any* writer wants to be caught dead in.

Nora Roberts, another multi-genre author who's dabbled in horror, has recently filed a lawsuit against a Brazilian writer, Christiane Serruya, for blatant plagiarism after readers saw glaring resemblances between the two authors' works. Roberts, who is a "household name" author, claimed for damages 3,000 times higher than Serruya's highest paying book on the list. Unfair? No. If you're going to undermine the work of any author by copying it word-for-word, you deserve to be sued and incarcerated. It is theft—intellectual theft remains theft. The point, however, is that Christiane Serruya, whether she *ever* releases an original novel under her own name or not, will forever be known as the writer who plagiarized Nora Roberts.

In the industry, her name is now damaged goods, besmirched by her own hand because she did not take the time to develop her own style, and was too lazy to come up with an original idea.

So how do you develop a writing style?

Writing styles develop and evolve naturally over time. They are influenced by your personality, your inspirations, and experiences. In other words, *you* are your writing style. There are, of course, some things you can do to develop your writing style other than sitting around and being awesome, though.

WRITE

Obviously the best way to develop your own signature style is by writing *a lot*. When you practice the craft, your payoff is honing a skill. *That* is admirable. Don't worry too much about what you're writing in the beginning. Just write whatever comes to mind. Embrace your deepest fears—the monster under the bed, a recurring nightmare of losing your teeth, falling from a great height—and describe your experiences. Practice makes perfect.

READ

Writers are usually veracious readers, because it teaches them the craft. Imagine your brain as a muscle and reading is the workout. Eventually, muscle memory kicks in, and you'll make fewer mistakes with spelling, grammar, and punctuation.

DON'T OVERTHINK WORDS

It's one thing to want to sound highly intelligent to readers, but be careful not to come across as pompous. If your demographic can't read your book without a dictionary, you're in trouble. Sometimes, the simpler word truly is a better choice.

EXPERIMENT

Experimenting with words develops your writing style. Rephrase long sentences until they are no longer awkward, because awkward prose pulls the reader out of the story. Try your hand at first-person narrative if you've only ever written third-person. Be creative and kill off a character in a ridiculous way. By experimenting, you're evolving. Your outrageous idea may not lead to a publishing contract immediately, but at least you're thinking out of the box.

The road to discovering who you truly are is not always an easy one. Sometimes, the process forces you to delve into your past. Admittedly, this isn't always a great place to be. Other times, you may have to relive experiences that are difficult. As cathartic as writing can be, dredging up the things we despise about ourselves and our lives can also make it impossible to put pen to paper. Still, those things, however bad they were, made you who you are today.

Another question you may be pondering is: How do you come up with an original idea? In truth, the best way to describe an original idea is by quoting the same thought, said in different ways, throughout the ages.

In Ecclesiastes 1:9 (NVT), it says:

"What has been will be again, what has been done will be done again; there is nothing new under the sun."

Arthur Conan Doyle wrote in *The Valley of Fear* that:

"Everything comes in circles. The old wheel turns, and the same spoke comes up. It's all been done before, and will be again."

Even Stanley Kubrick is quoted as saying:

"Everything has already been done. Every story has been told, every scene has been shot. It's our job to do it one better."

In other words, the same story *can* be retold countless times, but in order for it to work, you need to spin it in a way that makes it completely original, totally *you*. Vampire novels, for example, are the perfect way to explain how originality works. Bram Stoker wrote Dracula in 1897, but even then the idea of the undead wasn't new. He just made bloodsucking monsters a little sexier, and more palpable for the mainstream. Drawing inspiration from myths and legends, Stoker created something utterly his own, a classic horror novel that's spawned its own sub-genre. However, even those myths and legends were based upon something else—a question. Is there life after death? Of course, every author who's ever written a popular vampire novel has tackled some different theme in their exploration of the human condition; Anne Rice took the "little sexier" and amped it up to eleven in *Interview with the Vampire*, while Stephen King went much darker in *Salem's Lot*. From there, young adult classics were born, like: *The Vampire Diaries* by L.J. Smith, *Vampire Academy* by Richelle Mead, and of course everyone's favorite, *Twilight* by Stephanie Meyer. After seemingly every author in recent times has written a novel about vampires, it's easy to imagine the vampire is dead. The vampire, along with other horror tropes like the werewolf, zombie, ghost, and alien, is a hard sell to any publishing house, due to an oversaturated market. But one creative spark can breathe new life into the vampire at any time.

As great as it may be to be Stephen King, Clive Barker, Peter Straub, and Neil Gaiman, don't deny yourself the opportunity to step out of their shadows and turn your own fears into something everyone can enjoy.

Be you, a unique writer who learned the craft by studying the best, not by copying them.

Six Steps to Sustaining an Indie Career

Scott Nicholson

I am not sure anyone yet knows how to sustain an indie career in the digital era, despite some people who have been self-publishing since the dinosaur days of paper.

The only ones who have careers are those who are already closing in on their indie million. If it all ended tomorrow, they could probably manage okay with some smart investing.

Those who are getting a decent income right now could see it go one of two ways. If it ended tomorrow, a solid percentage would immediately shift to giving their books away to "build audience," even if a paying audience down the road seems unlikely. Those who quit their day jobs to go indie can probably find other jobs, and have a great story for the grandkids about when they were "real authors." A few will continue to parlay indie success into a corporate career.

But even corporate careers are tough to sustain, with only a minority of lucky authors getting those third and fourth book deals and then building a long-term career. And, if the indie era collapsed, one would suspect those same factors would probably make an even more dramatic impact on publishers with much higher overheads.

While it's difficult to predict how everything will turn out, your chances of surviving either way are best if you continue to run your writing like both an art and a business, like so:

1. Continue to write, no matter what. Without products, you have no options.

2. Expand your markets. You're on Kindle. Great. So are a quarter-million other authors, and that number is expanding daily. So get on Nook, Smashwords, Kobo, and everywhere else, and try to develop sales at your own site—the only site where you will be guaranteed to maintain control and a suitable royalty, as well as avoid competing with the scammers who seem to proliferate like bacteria.

3. Consider diversifying your genres. You don't know what the next trend will be. If you don't find trends artistically satisfying, write what you like and hope the market catches up. While branding is helpful, it is also limiting. If you are prolific, consider a pen name—but a pen name is probably wasted on a one-shot, so unless you are going to establish the pen name as its own brand, avoid it.

4. Pay attention to the markets. Try to anticipate and stay ahead of the curve, whether on pricing, content, covers, devices, or what readers want. At the same time, develop your business skills. A great marketer will beat the pants off a great writer nine times out of ten.

5. Keep building your network. Having more friends makes writing more fun, but be careful you don't spend

more time tweeting than writing. As the digital revolution evolves, you might see new opportunities open that you hadn't considered—everything from ad-supported e-books to shared-adventure stories to translation opportunities.

6. Take chances. In any evolutionary leap, a number of critters are left behind. Usually they are the ones who are slowest to adapt, often because they are following the herd, which means they are the last to get to the vital resources and the first to fall prey to predators. Extinction is the result.

Most of all, enjoy the journey. A number of indie writers seem unhappy because they have expectations and are disappointed because they aren't one of the indie lottery winners. Be grateful for this incredible opportunity. If this is as good as it ever gets, that's still pretty darned good! If you don't believe me, try talking to oldtimers like me who broke in during the 1980s and 1990s and could paper a garage with rejection slips—yes, paper rejection slips received through the postal mail. Clicking a button and making your book available around the world is a modern miracle. You're lucky to be here.

An Interview with Stephen Graham Jones

Joe Mynhardt

Joe Mynhardt: Let's start off with the horror genre itself. What makes it so appealing for so many of us? And even more so why in the written format?

Stephen Graham Jones: I think there's just a whole lot of us who are wired for the visceral reaction horror provokes. But it's not about desensitized, needing harder and harsher stimuli—that always feels like an accusation, an indictment. Or, it's sure not a compliment, anyway, right? Just, some of us like the rush of turning all the lights off at the bottom of some cave system, and some really don't like that at all. Me, I think I probably don't just love having those lights off, being lost in that inky velvety darkness, but I do very much like the way I smile when the lights finally come back on. That's what I like about horror: the laughter after. Of being alive—of being, now, *more* alive. As for print media versus visual…I mean, the trick with print is that, first, it's a lot more portable, doesn't necessarily require batteries, but there's a difference in flavor too, isn't there? Like, on the page there's less jumpscares, more dread, and, because you're having to live with a novel three or four days to read it, say, then it can etch itself deeper into your head, I think, maybe because you're kind of a participant, a co-creator.

Joe: Do you have any advice for authors who find themselves overwhelmed with trying to balance writing with their daily responsibilities?

Stephen: First, those writers aren't alone. Those writers are all of us. But, my own rule is that after family and health, writing always has precedence. So, not the bar, not watching sports, not reality television, not mowing the lawn, and not all the 'responsibilities' the world's always foisting on us. I used to have three things, too, something other than family and health, but I've since calved off whatever that other thing was. But, that isn't advice. Here, advice: steal every moment you can, and don't over-ritualize your writing. You know how some parents won't be quiet while their baby's sleeping, as they don't want to train it to need that absolute silence? That's what we need to do as writers: train ourselves so that all we need to write is five minutes—not the light this way instead of that way, not this lucky robe, not this or that room, whatever hour, and not only after you've processed through some checklist. Just sit down and go, wherever you are, however you are. Stolen time, time I'm stealing from myself, when I know I should be doing something else, that's when I get the absolute most done. But, yeah, a world of us adhering to that isn't that great a world. But, ten percent of us not mowing the lawn, just staying at the keyboard and playing with dragons? I think that's just fine.

Joe: Let's look at the psyche of the horror writer for a bit. What do you think makes him/her tick? Makes them different from everyone else.

Stephen: Most will say they saw *The Exorcist* too early, or read some Stephen King before they were really old enough. Which is kind of saying that one early perturbation, and here I am, ta-daa. You can't really deny that, either. But? Wonder if they'd be writing the gory stuff anyway, without having seen Regan's head twist, without having read whatever King? No way to know. I don't know what makes everybody else tick, but this horror writer, me, what makes me tick is that I'm perpetually scared. I'm always thinking there's a ghost standing behind me, I'm always thinking the aliens must have abducted me last night, and put me back together pretty poorly, judging by how junky my ankles and knees are working this morning. And taking the trash out at night? That's just asking for a werewolf or zombie to jump me. So, I mean, I guess I see monsters and danger everywhere, pretty much. Makes sense that I'd write what I know.

Joe: Which aspect(s) of writing (voice, characterization, setting, mood, show vs. tell, dialogue etc.) would you place the most importance on and why?

Stephen: Easy: voice. But by 'voice' I don't mean diction or style. To me voice is the set of rules the story's going to use to tell itself. It's the license it claims in its very first utterance. Story premises are a dime a dozen—no a dime for a *hundred*—but the right voice to activate a premise, that's gold, man, that's some rare stuff. Ideas are easy.

Methods of delivery can be nearly impossible. They're not something you can muscle onto the page, either. You just luck into them. Or, that's the way it works for me, anyway. I write and write, just spinning my wheels, going nowhere, and then something clicks, and everything organizes around that, and then I'm off and running. This doesn't always happen at the keyboard, either. Often as not, it's when I'm out and about, doing stuff with my hands, not meaning to be thinking about this story problem. But your mind's always trying to figure it out. If you don't over-direct it, it usually can. Thinking, to me, is the worst thing for writing. Give me instinct and luck any day instead.

Joe: As a former educator, I understand all too well the importance of dissecting and studying a problem or obstacle, but how should an author find the balance between letting their creative minds free and treating the writing craft as a science to be studied.

Stephen: Best I can do in the writing classroom is relay my own experience, not lay down absolutes. Well, except stuff like we really-really need independent clauses after semicolons, or direct-address commas are actually necessary, not a matter of style. But, I can tell students that this probably won't work, that I've never seen it work, that I've done it myself and failed hard, but? Go ahead, try it, sure. Maybe you'll be the one who pulls it off. But, really, with writing, you learn the most simply from writing, not necessarily from instruction. So, making the students write, and write and write and write, that's the best I can do for them. Aside from correcting their punctuation. But, industry stuff, that's where a publishing writing instructor can help the most, I think. Learning the ins and outs of publishing is a trial-and-error affair, but I can jump the student over a lot of that, I think. I wish when I was coming up I'd known a lot of the industry-stuff I know now. Hard-earned kind of knowledge, which I'm always happy to pass on. They've got to ask the right questions, though, just because I don't always know what I know.

A Good Story

Lucy A. Snyder

Earlier this year, I asked Facebook friends to leave comments if they (or those they love to read) are queer horror authors. It was a popular post. While remarks like "Me! I'm gay!" or "Heck yes! Clive Barker is my favorite!" dominated the thread, there were also several comments like this: "I don't care about the author's sexuality; *I just want a good story.*"

A good story. Doesn't every reader of popular fiction want that? And that plea for a good story seems pretty broad-minded at first glance, doesn't it? These readers are all about the narrative! It doesn't matter if we writers are black or white, male or female, liberal or conservative, gay or straight! Story is queen.

Story is royally critical, no question. But it doesn't exist in a vacuum separate from the writer. Writing good fiction isn't like baking cookies or assembling a model car kit. It's *personal.* We write what we know. Our hopes, our dreams, our fears, our obsessions, our experiences…it's all material for our tales. We horror writers are cutting ourselves open and spreading ourselves out there on the page.

Any given story of mine is a mix of the completely imaginary and the deeply intimate. And that's true for any other horror or dark fantasy author in service to his or her craft. A reasonably attentive reader of my fiction could guess that I'm either queer or am thinking a whole lot of queer thoughts.

Horror is the literature of fear. And if you're queer, and if you write fiction about your darkest fears while also doing your very best to tell a good story, a funny thing happens. Many of those readers who claimed to just care about story are now all squirmy. Sure, the plot's exciting…but you made it all weird! Why couldn't you just write a good old-fashioned entertaining story where the monsters are uncomplicatedly monstrous and the heroic guy gets the trophy girl at the end? Why couldn't your story be *straight,* darn it?

All of us who write horror have to find that middle road between art and commerce. Satisfying art means striving to meet a high craft standard for our work while being true to ourselves, but satisfying commerce means producing a piece of writing that will sell. Those two goals are not mutually exclusive, but the further your writing strays from what readers and publishers are comfortable with, the more difficult it is to reconcile the two.

LGBTQ authors have made tremendous strides into the mainstream in the past few decades. But our cultural image of the average person is still someone who's straight, white, and male, with the emphasis on straight. And that cultural default can affect publishers' perceptions of the kinds of characters readers want to see in their books.

The only time I've *ever* argued with an editor's request for revisions was when one asked me to straighten the female protagonist of one of my stories. This was just a few years ago, and the tale was for a horror anthology aimed at adults and teens. Here are the relevant parts of the email he sent me:

> *[Publisher Redacted] will have a hard time with a few issues that I think are easily fixed and really don't have that much bearing on the story.*

> *The second thing, and I know it is very subtle with no action, is the lesbian aspect. I don't have a problem with it myself, but at the same time, I think you would have a stronger character if she was straight…*

> *The reason [Publisher Redacted] will have a problem is (honestly) their personal beliefs, and the contracts they have with local school systems, which purchase large quantities of books.*

While I appreciated his candor—it's likely I'd had stories rejected for queer themes before but the editors wouldn't be straight about it—my jaw was on the floor.

My story's viewpoint character was a violent survivor; her love for her partner was the only remnant of her humanity, and that love was at the core of all her motivations. The only way my zombie-slaying, bandit-murdering, weapons-stealing protagonist would be a "stronger" heroine as a heterosexual…would be if queerness is a defect.

So, I wrote him back:

> *I'm glad you enjoyed the story. I can change the magic details, no problem there. But I have personal objections to straightening my character to make her more acceptable. I'm sad that you would ask that of me (I'm queer). Lesbian, gay, and bisexual children and teens exist (and make up a nontrivial portion of the kids who read SF and fantasy) just as black and*

Hispanic and Asian teens exist, and asking me to make a lesbian character straight to make her acceptable is not any different than asking me to make a black character white for the sake of a publisher who thinks black people bear the mark of Cain.

And as for the books being purchased by schools— gay and lesbian characters regularly appear in YA and middle grade books that appear in libraries and schools around the country; I just don't see that having a lesbian character is really that unusual these days: "There are so many queer characters in YA lit now, including manga and graphic novels, that the topic doesn't seem nearly as controversial as it once did. At conferences and conventions where educators and librarians gather, there are always sessions with LGBTQ topics. Inclusiveness is all the rage." (see bit.ly/lo_afterellen for the whole article).

I do want to be a part of the book. I am willing to make some changes to make her orientation more subtle, but I won't straighten her. I hope you will reconsider your request in that regard.

He wrote me back with a heartfelt apology, but made it clear that business concerns trumped everything else:

The school system orders these books for every student (in specific grades) in the county. I assure you it is a large purchase and projects are cultivated to fit into this program. The County Commission actually purchases the books…they have a board that approves the books before they are purchased. They are very strict. …[Publisher Redacted] can't afford the projects without the County Commission purchases. Therefore, if they turn down a project, the project will not make it to the light of day.

The subtext I read was, "Don't be difficult, Lucy. This is just how the world works. Obviously, brain-fiending zombies and plagues and murder and decapitations are good clean fun as far as the school system is concerned. But a woman feeling romantic love for another woman? Heavens no! They *have* to think of the children!"

After my initial flush of frustration at his response, I started thinking of my own childhood. I went through my first suicidal depression at the age of twelve. If I'd been just a little more resourceful, a little less fearful, I would not be here right now. I would not have written this column or anything else.

Why was I suicidal? I felt completely isolated and unwanted and defective. I was fat. I was a nerd. I was weird in so many ways. And deep down, I knew I was queer.

Being queer was the worst. I couldn't admit it to anyone, not even myself. Back then in that little dust-blown town in Texas, queers were at best morally weak crazy people who needed years of shameful psychiatry to straighten out. At worst, they were perverts and predators, innately evil and not really human. If someone killed a queer, well, that wasn't what proper law-abiding folks did, but it was still doing the world a favor, wasn't it?

I escaped into books. I could pretend to be someone else for a while, someone who mattered in their world and had amazing adventures in fabulous places. All those characters I wanted to be were arrow-straight, and mostly male. While I got temporary comfort from these novels, they ultimately reinforced the image I had of myself as being defective because I wasn't a boy (and therefore wouldn't ever do anything really cool) and I wasn't like the other girls, either. Not at all. I was something else, something nobody wanted around. Something that probably didn't deserve to be alive.

So when I hear someone tell me that characters have to be heterosexual to keep them fit for younger readers? I'm hearing that person tell me that the world was a right and proper place when it made me want to commit suicide before I'd even turned teen.

If I'd had queer female protagonists in my books? They would have been signs that there *might* be a future where I belonged and could be happy. I'd have still had plenty of problems as a fat nerdy kid who consistently failed to perform her gender correctly. But I'd have felt I deserved to breathe air.

Despite my self-loathing, I didn't kill myself. A decade later I escaped to a college town that tolerated gays and lesbians. Life got better. Eventually I came to grips with my own queerness. I wrote hard, and earned myself a career as a professional horror writer.

Being a pro writer is as integral to my public identity as my sexuality is to my private identity. And when you're a pro, you make the sale. When an editor who's offering you hard cash tells you to change something, you change it.

Even if it means you wouldn't be able to look your twelve-year-old self in the eye.

Even if it means you can't really look your grown-up self in the eye, either, because you just erased your own existence from your story. For six cents a word.

But this is America, and while story is queen…business is king. So I did the best I could: I made the queer aspects of the character as subtle as anything you'd find in a 1950s film hiding in the celluloid closet. The editor accepted my rewrite, and life went on.

The good news is that since then, I haven't had another editor reject a story for containing queer characters or themes. For instance, Jason Sizemore operates Apex Publications from Kentucky and frequently calls himself a hillbilly. Despite the socially conservative climate in his state, he's supported LGBTQ authors and he originally published my Stoker-winning queer tale "Magdala Amygdala."

So, publishers who want to be allies and see the value in publishing diverse voices are managing to do that just fine. Hopefully before too long we'll be living in a world where other publishers' beliefs (whether about religion or reader expectations) and County Commissions across the land aren't keeping queer characters out of books and limiting the scope of human stories that readers get to choose from.

And then, we can all be sure that it's really the story that matters.

Writing Dialogue

Richard Thomas

There are many components that go into a great story. You need to have a layered, vivid setting. You need to create a narrative hook that pulls your audience in and a story that keeps them interested. You need characters that are complex, flawed, and realistic. And you need dialogue that rings true.

FUNCTION OF DIALOGUE

Why do we use dialogue in our stories? Like everything else in your fiction, it should move the story forward, give us information, or reveal character. It can help to foreshadow events, reveal a vivid setting, and show us deep, layered relationships. If you aren't doing some (or all) of these things with your dialogue, then you aren't using all of the tools in your tool belt. So how do you do that?

LISTEN

Whenever you are out and about, or even watching television, movies, or listening to the radio, be more aware of how people talk. Most people are pretty casual about how they speak. Absorb conversations at coffee shops, write it down if you want—take notes at bars and clubs, family gatherings. And watch how people react. You can put all of that into your writing, and your dialogue.

CONTRACTIONS

Most of the time you'll want to use contractions in your dialogue, people aren't as formal as you may think. See, right there. I said "you'll" not "you will" as well as "aren't" instead of "are not." Now, if your character is an 18th century baron, maybe he speaks in a more formal tone, or if you are writing about a character where this fits, even in contemporary times, current day, by all means speak that way. But most of the time you should use contractions.

BREAK IT UP WITH ACTION

Long lines of dialogue are fine, but I wouldn't go more than a few exchanges back and forth without adding in some lines that tell more of the story, reveal what is happening, the physical action, all five senses, the thoughts of your narrator or characters, etc. It's also easy for your readers to get lost, even if you constantly tag your dialogue with he/she said or Bob/Mary said. When you show us what is happening, it does those three things I mentioned above: moves the story forward, gives us information, or reveals character.

Two people are talking about an affair a friend had, smoking cigarettes, drinking bourbon. We want to hear them say the words, "I knew she was fooling around," but we also want to see a hand run through unkempt hair, fingers drumming on the table, eyes darting to the attractive bartender as she rubs a glass dry, over and over again.

TAGS

99 percent of the time, all you need is he said, or she said. That's it. "That's not my shrunken head," he said. "Well, it's not mine, either" she said, tossing the dry, brittle skull in the air, a grin spreading over her face.

ACTION TAGS

Dialogue and then action—or if you're feeling brave, action tags. Now, I don' t mean those horrible Tom Swifties. You know what those are? "We just struck oil!" Tom gushed. Or, "Pass me the shellfish," Tom said crabbily. Those are terrible, right? But if you think you can handle it, and I challenge you to push yourself, add action tags to your dialogue—it can show you what is happening in a powerful way. But if you say, "I don't know," Jim shrugged, we get more on body, physical information. Those little beats, those breaks—revealing a blush of skin, a hand gesture, usually something physical—they will add to the scene, grounding the words in reality.

PUNCTUATION

This goes without saying, but know how to use your commas and quotations marks. I'm sure you all have it down by now. Refer to a guide, Strunk and White, if you need to. Make sure you capitalize where it's needed, get your commas inside the quotation marks, all of that obvious stuff. Once you get used to it, you won't even think about it anymore.

INTERRUPT

I personally hate ellipses...a lot. But find a way to interrupt your dialogue, because people do that. I prefer em-dashes. Think about the last fight you had with a spouse, friend, or family member. Did you wait for the other person to stop speaking so you could have your say? Do children always wait patiently to speak? I'm a much bigger fan of fragments than ellipses.

"But—"
"Shut up, Roddy," she said.
"Mary...wait."
"I'm not waiting anymore. For anyone."
"But—"
"No but, no nothing. Not anymore."
"Please," he said. "Listen to me."
"I'm done listening," she said.

Something like that might work.

SLANG

Be sure to use slang, where appropriate. People use words like "dude, man, yeah," all the time. Sprinkle it into your dialog. SPRINKLE, I say. Unless a character has a chorus, a voice that begs for it, you could end up sounding like Beavis and Butthead or Jeff Spicoli.

STEREOTYPES

Be careful about writing characters that are dull and obvious—avoid stereotypes. Is every mafia don a fat Italian man? Is every inner city criminal a muscular black guy? Is every woman in distress a buxom blonde? Whatever your characters, try going against type. That's why Mike Tyson is so hilarious, that high-pitched, lisping voice. It's not at all the Barry White voice you'd expect from a boxer. But then again, a dockworker in Brooklyn or Baltimore may really speak in a certain way, with stereotypical language and word choices. So if you go that route, find a way to mix it up. A factory worker that always tries to use big words, that can become an amusing trait—or it can reveal a hidden intellect that shows us how dangerous he really is.

READ IT OUT LOUD

One of the best ways to check your dialogue is to read it out loud. Wherever you stumble—mark it, and fix it. Is it your word choice, the phrasing, the way you break the dialogue apart, does it need more/less tags—all of that. Listen to the words you say and think about who is speaking. Does the mousy librarian say, "Get out of my fucking library, you assholes!" or does she say, "Get out of my precious library, you hooligans." Think about region— are you in the north, south, east, or west? Is your character highly educated or a dropout, living on the street? Their status, their history, their current situation (drunk, angry, dying, lost, scared) will dictate how they speak.

CONCLUSION

In the end, dialogue has to ring true. In addition to moving the story forward ("I slept with your wife.") giving us information ("And that thing, with her tongue, did you teach her that?") and revealing character ("I liked it.") your dialogue has to be believable. It can't pull us out of the story. It can't break character, unless done really well. A cold-blooded killer that suddenly shows a soft side on the last page, scooping up a kitten and whispering sweet nothings in her ear—no, that probably won't work. The same killer that early on quotes poetry in private, tends a flower garden, and helps at his church—then, at the end picks up that same kitten and mutters nonsense to it—that may work. Read it out loud, listen to the words, and ask yourself, "Does this sound right? Would I say that? Do I believe this?" Trust your instincts, your gut. In time, it will all be second nature.

The Hitchhiking Effect

Gene O'Neill

In the summer of 1979 I spent six weeks at Clarion, which at that time was located at Michigan State University in East Lansing. It was one of the most intense six weeks in my life (*almost* comparable to the first part of Marine Corps boot camp).

It was the first time I'd been away from my young family for any extended period of time. It was my first time meeting a professional writer. It was the first time reading any unpublished writing other than my own. It was the first time anyone had ever critiqued my writing. It was the first time I'd heard the term, "plot skeleton." So, I soaked up everything and learned so many things about writing and the life of being a writer…Perhaps the most important thing I learned was how to read my own material with a critical, objective eye, and then to make the necessary cuts, additions, and revisions after going over the writing again and again and again. (What Hemingway called exercising the BS Detector)

At the end of Clarion I was not in the top of my group of eighteen colleagues in terms of skill and writer development, but, I must have demonstrated a spark of talent, because Damon Knight and Kate Wilhelm invited me to attend the monthly gatherings of writers at their home in Eugene, Oregon. I lived in Northern California, about an eight-hour drive away, but I was highly motivated to take advantage of the opportunity to learn more. They suggested I might get along with a young writer, Stan Robinson, who lived near me in Davis, California. Stan and I would make the trip up to Eugene eight or nine times during 1980. And like Damon and Kate suspected, the two of us got along fabulously. We became good friends.

Our routine: I'd drive over to Davis around 5:30 on Saturday morning, pick up Stan, and then we would power up to Eugene and arrive in the early afternoon, just in time to hunker down and read all the manuscripts that were scheduled to be critiqued that night.

I learned a lot during those weekends in Eugene—perhaps as much on those eight or nine marathon trips during 1980, as I learned full time at Clarion. We met a number of amazing young writers in Oregon, some who would soon become very well-known—John Shirley, William Gibson, Lucius Shepherd, Vonda McIntire, Steve Perry, Mark Laidlaw, and several others. Somewhere early on, maybe the fifth or so trip up, I took along a new short story entitled, "The Burden of Indigo." I knew it must be good, because Stan broke the rule that we never talked in the car about material we were taking up for the Clarion-style group critique. He said some very enthusiastic nice things. As did most of the others in Eugene—a rare thing, as the group was usually a very harsh critic of stuff. But Damon brought me back to earth with his sarcastic take on a critical scene in the story—he said the description of a young boy sitting by a pond reminded him of a *cherub on a religious postcard*. I transferred his criticism literally and incorporated it directly into the short story—the main character thinks the boy looks like "a cherub on a postcard." In the kitchen later that night I knew I had made an important step as a writer—that moment when you *know* you have crossed over from being a typist to being a writer. Kate said to me in the kitchen after the critique, "I knew that you had something to say." That was all she said, but it was enough.

I was to learn as much from Stan Robinson during the eight hours in the car up and the eight hours back—we rapped on all the time (at that time we likened ourselves to the beats making one of their marathon trips). Stan was formally educated—an English/Writing major. He would soon go down to UC San Diego and finish his PhD. And although we would often communicate, I lost my only first reader. On those long trips, he passed on a ton of the formal writing tips/theory that I'd missed by not formally studying English, Literature, or Writing in college. And I would arrive back home exhausted, but immediately jot down what I'd been exposed to both in Eugene and by Stan during the weekend (For example, I'd never heard the term and importance of a story's *premise*. I also heard Stan's theory that an expository lump was just fine…if it was interesting—a contrast to what I'd been told at Clarion. We talked of future projects, and I heard the complete outline for the Mars Trilogy years before they were written).

Information in the car didn't travel only one-way, though. I'd had a pretty well rounded street education by then, beginning from the time I grew up in a working-class ghetto near a shipyard—boxing and playing other sports— to holding a number of blue collar jobs, serving in the Marines overseas, working my way slowly through a small

State college in Sacramento, and eventually teaching Adaptive P.E. Stan, to his credit, took note of much of that *colorful* street stuff, even including relevant bits in his own writing. When he won a first Nebula for his novella, *The Blind Geometer*, he mentioned one of his characters was informed and provided a great role model by a real life P.E. teacher.

So the trips up and back were a major learning experience and influence on my development as a writer. But something I heard in passing in Eugene I stored away, and it would eventually inform the quality of my writing in a *major* way.

Kate Wilhelm, during one of those weekends, had briefly suggested in conversation that she thought *all* writing, including your fiction, was autobiographical in some way. At the time I completely dismissed that idea. After all, at the time I was writing and would soon publish mostly a kind of hybrid science fiction—with off worlds, aliens, and some of the other tropes of SF. To me this material obviously wasn't autobiographical.

But it's interesting how things stick in the back of your mind for years.

As time passed, my writing gradually matured, and I became more solidly a mixed-genre writer, even occasionally turning out a mainstream piece of fiction (this was hard to sell at the time—another story). But at some point, I began to wonder if Kate's suggestion might not be actually profound. After due consideration, I had to admit that an important component in *each* of my best stories was the right-on, emotional reactions of the characters. I realized that the reliability and validity of those emotional reactions came from a life-long experiment involving only one Subject—the experimental S was me of course. So, I carefully read back over all my previous published work, even the more-or-less early SF, and I eventually realized that Kate was probably correct. I found large pieces of myself in almost every story, often in the emotional reactions of the main characters—both male and female, gay and straight, good guy and bad guy, whomever. At some point in each piece of that early work—sometimes in several places—I found a direct parallel with my own life experiences.

For example, my first professional sale was to The Twilight Zone Magazine, a mixed-genre story, "The Burden of Indigo." Readers have commented on realistically sharing the *feelings* of the Indigo Man, his lonely sense of isolation and being ostracized by both Shield residents and Freemen. When I was seven, I had polio, and spent nine months partially paralyzed in a bed at San Francisco Children's Hospital. After making an amazing full recovery, I returned to my grandparent's home near the naval shipyard. At that time people were frightened by a lack of understanding of polio—much like the early fear of AIDS. The working class in my neighborhood thought it was an indication of being dirty and not sanitary, being *low* class. I was mostly ostracized and left alone, *except* when I had to defend myself when being tormented and attacked on the way home after school.

Ironically at this time, the doctors recommended to my Grams that I spend my afternoons lying down and resting in my bedroom for at least an hour. I hated this restriction and of course never slept. Instead, I made up stories about the shadows flickering on my bedroom walls, when the Venetian blinds were partially closed (Damon said that all writers were little green frogs sometime in their life history, and I was during that time). Later on, perhaps as a reaction to this rough and tumble early time, I would develop a strong interest and more than just a little expertise in contact sports, like football, basketball, and boxing. Even now the memory of those lonely times back when I was eight or nine still cause an emotional reaction (I feel for that little boy).

Okay, what did I do with this discovery about my own writing? Down through the last thirty or so years, I've made a *conscious* effort to capitalize on this observation.

Whenever appropriate during the story development, I insert some true-life event/character, trying to capture my own emotional response in words and transfer them to the page. If I've selected the correct words and efficiently completed the transfer to the page, the reader should experience the emotional content of the scene. Of course, usually I'm only partially successful, but the piece may still turn out to be pretty good. Sometimes, I'm not talented enough to encapsulate *any* of the real poignancy I feel into words (romantic material perhaps becoming too sentimental). Or maybe something that caused a deep impact in my real life didn't always translate too well, didn't emotionally move the reader despite my writing ability (a harsh observation from the ghetto, or something in the boxing ring, or from my Marine experience—the violence perhaps not believable or too shocking, masking whatever intimacy I hoped to share).

As one might expect, I often had to disguise the real life event. Damon used to say, you will *never* be a very good writer until you can strip naked and pirouette in front of your audience. I take this to mean the very good writer takes chances, *no* flinching. Or something similar to what Hemingway meant when he said that, *The good writer like the good bullfighter fights in the terrain of the bullfighter; but the great writer like the great bullfighter fights in the terrain of the bull.* I've reached the point in my writing life where I have no problem figuratively shucking off my clothes and dancing—I don't worry about reader judgments of my personal preferences/behaviors they assume from my writing. But I can't, in good conscience, strip away all the clothes of a relative, colleague, or friend. So the actual scene transferred may itself sometimes be a kind of fiction, but its structure *true*, nonetheless.

Those parts of my writing, where the reader is able to pick up on the emotional transference and be truly moved, are often recognized as my better work. And I would usually agree with the assessment.

I call what I attempt to do *The hitchhiking effect*— transferring the emotional load of an autobiographical experience from my own background directly into my fiction writing for the reader to hitchhike on. This seems to work well for me.

Nowadays, I would fully agree with Kate Wilhelm that my fiction is indeed autobiographical.

The Horror Network

Jess Landry

S o, you're at a point where you're finally comfortable (even a little) calling yourself a writer. First off, congratulations! You've taken that dive off the deep end in writing: you've written a story/novel/collection/script/what have you (or multiple)— you've accomplished something that not many can do.

But with a few cats in the bag, you may find yourself asking, *now what? What can I do not only to promote my work, but to get my own name out there?*

A career (or even a hobby) in writing often goes beyond simply putting pen to paper—you need to build your brand. Now, this is not an essential practice for writers as there are the occasional few who've escaped any sort of branding and that have garnered decent popularity of sorts (Thomas Ligotti comes to mind), but in this day and age, it certainly doesn't hurt to put yourself out there so people may recognize your name.

There are a lot of different factors that go into creating your brand (cost, readiness, general hatred of the human population) and everyone is different, so if you do put stock into these tips, do only what feels right to you.

1. Get ready to mingle

Sure, writing is mostly a solitary sport, but there may come a time when trading in your sweat pants for something not as comfortable could serve you well. In or around a big city? Chances are you're near some sort of writing event— take advantage of everything it has to offer, if it's within your budget and comfort zone (even if something isn't your cup of tea—take a risk. You never know if it could pay off). Take classes, go to speaking events, put yourself out there and grow your name in your community. Who knows, you could be asked to participate in your town's next writers festival (or maybe you'll start your own). No festivals near you? How about a convention? There are many great speculative-related cons around the world (StokerCon, which changes cities, and sometimes countries, every year; NecromoniCon; Fan Expo Canada)—do some digging online to see what's near you.

2. Get ready to mingle (digitally)

Now here's something you *can* do in your sweat pants—get your name out there online. The best place to start is on social media (it's not all Russian bots and dick pics— honest!). Follow, friend, and poke like-minded individuals, pages, organizations, venues, whatever piques your interest. Interact with all your newfound digital buddies, don't just be a lurker in the shadows. Post questions, come up with your wittiest comments, engage your audience. But give people breathing room—try not to flood your friends with messages or page like requests or post every hour of every day (unless it's animal photos, then please do post every hour of every day). Do everything in moderation, and you'll be just fine.

Another good place to get your foot in the door (and also a great way to practice your craft) is to review books. Sites like Hellnotes, Cemetery Dance, and others always have the latest and greatest takes on the hottest releases, so reach out to see if any sites are accepting new reviewers. Taking apart novels, movies, and video games will only give you better insight on how to craft your own stories—you'll be able to see what works for you and what doesn't. You also might end up discovering a new favourite author or getting your hands on an advance reading copy (ARC) of a popular upcoming release.

3. Join an organization

For a blossoming writer, joining a writing organization allows you to meet others in the exact same boat as you—others looking to boost their names and expand their horizons. Many organizations offer great incentives for the up-and-coming writer, and there is no other name in horror than the Horror Writers Association. The organization offers a mentorship program aimed at pairing seasoned pros with those starting out. Scholarship funds are available to both non-members and members, and are given out specifically for poets, female-identifying authors, and non-fiction writers, among others. The organization also throws one of the biggest, baddest parties of the year—StokerCon. Here, they offer panels, classes, and networking opportunities, all wrapped up by the Bram Stoker Awards ceremony where the lucky few go home with a haunted house statue. The organization offers membership levels for all levels of writers—from beginners (Supporting), to current pros (Active), and Academics. Check out horror.org to see everything the HWA offers.

4. Small presses

If the opportunity arises for you to work behind the scenes for a small press (or any sized press, really), and should you be interested in seeing what goes into creating a book from start to finish, then this is the way to go. If not, stop reading here. It's okay, I won't take offence.

Signing on to work for a press is all guts, no glory. You'll work tirelessly (and tiredly) with authors while you help them achieve their dreams. It can be extremely satisfying, if you have the time and the willingness. You'll learn the ins and outs of publishing, which could help you in the future with your own projects. And you'll likely meet a lot of amazing people along the way, people you can always look to later in life for guidance or a small favour or two.

If you find that you're really into the business side of things, then why not start your own press? Get to know everything you need to know, then publish the books you want to publish. There's no lack of great writers out there, waiting for that golden opportunity. And plenty of people who own indie publishing houses are writers themselves.

5. Seek out others

What better way to grow your network than with others in the same predicament as you? You're all scared shitless, shivering in the same boat, wondering what the hell to do next, so why not suffer together? Form a writing group, be it online or in-person. Read each other's work. Offer helpful critiques. Suggest open calls that may not be your thing, but could be someone else's. When one of your gang succeeds, celebrate them. When one fails, hold them up. We're a unique bunch, us writers—we mostly enjoy the solitude, but it helps knowing there are others wondering the same things that you are, be it about your story idea, structure, or if the FBI has tapped into your Google searches. Find your tribe. And as your group grows, so will you.

6. Seek out other opportunities

Don't limit yourself to writing one genre or one type of story. Get those hands dirty and search for writing opportunities until you reach the end of the internet, from freelancing gigs to one-offs. Opportunities could vary from online to in-person, from paying to non-paying (which sucks, but you often have to start somewhere), from permanent to one every now and again. If you want them, then seize those shots. Take on anything you can handle (and some that you think you can't)—not only will you get your name out there, you'll also gain valuable experience that can only help you grow as a writer.

Of course, another way to get your name out there is simply to write and start submitting. Submit long. Submit hard. But make sure your work is polished, and that you follow the submission guidelines of the venue you're submitting to.

There is no perfect combination to networking. Just as with writing, it's a lot of hard work, and for a lot of authors, it doesn't come easily. And, as with everything in life, there are no guarantees. But if you stick with it and believe in yourself, you can achieve whatever it is you set out to do. At the end of the day, do what makes you happy. And if that's just being able to write and not having to deal with anything else, then you know what? Just write.

Interview with David Owain Hughes

Joe Mynhardt

Joe Mynhardt: How did your fascination with the horror genre start, and what about it continues to draw you in?

David Owain Hughes: My fascination with the horror genre began when I was young. I was around five years old, and when my older brothers would babysit me on Saturday night, they would rent horror flicks from our local video shop. And back then of course, in the early eighties, there was a boom in the horror film genre and the whole 'Video Nasties' thing erupted in the U.K. Yeah, the British government sure did play hell, and stripped the worst of the worst horror flicks from off the shelves of every video shop they could.

I'm deviating.

So, yeah, my brothers would rent these awful movies and I'd be in my pre-adolescent element. Hell, it got to a point where I was asking for bloodier flicks. The bloodier the better. I guess I couldn't get enough, not that I remember, mind. Weird child, right? And it wasn't just horror, either, even though a fondness had settled. Nope, I loved ninja and pirate movies and anything that had a cool and scary violent element to them.

But what's cooler than monsters, right? Especially zombies. And werewolves. My first true monster loves. Which brings me to the first few horror films I was ever exposed to at that tender age of five: *The Howling Part 2* and Sam Raimi's *Evil Dead* trilogy.

Lots of others followed: *Critters, Ghoulies, Maniac Cop,* the entire *Friday the 13th* franchise, etcetera. The eighties were ripe with picking. It was great. A true golden age.

From there, my interest in the genre kept growing. And the rest, as they say, is history.

Joe: It's easy for authors to fall into bouts of depression, especially when we write about the dark stuff for too long. How do you balance your writing with keeping yourself in a positive frame of mind?

David: Fighting depression is hard. There is no easy solution to this one sadly (not for me, anyway), so keeping a positive frame of mind is difficult at times.

At the beginning of this year, I made it public that I suffer from mental health issues, and that I was setting out on a path to seek professional help. I think finally being truthful with myself that there was a problem was a huge step in the right direction. It also helped me to open up and talk to my wife, which was another massive positive. I wouldn't say it saved my relationship, because Nicola is an amazing woman who stood by me, but it definitely helped solidify us further. Unloading all my baggage on her was such a relief. I didn't want her living with a stranger. I always promised myself that when I got married, my wife would know everything.

Joe: What are the signs of depression we need to look out for, not just as human beings, but authors who tend to spend a lot of time with our own thoughts?

David: I'm not so sure the signs for depression are the same for everyone, but I have a few that lead to mine, such as lack of sleep. This is probably my biggest sign that a depressive episode is imminent, and the most triggered, which I can't always avoid by just having a nap. Life isn't as simple as that, sadly, as there are things that must be done: school run, work, deadlines, etcetera. Having said that, I have learned to take myself off to bed where and when I can if things are starting to bear down on me. This is something I've had to work on because I don't like taking naps, as it messes with my main sleep.

Lack of sleep usually leads me to dark places. The mind turns, plays tricks on me, and makes me think of things I don't want to think of, such as my past and the rest of the useless luggage my brain seems to carry around. It also makes me doubt myself and think I'm a complete failure at everything, including life. Once I'm in that black hole, I can be there for weeks. Hell, I've seen depressive episodes last months.

If it's not lack of sleep that propels me into the aforementioned hole, then it's procrastination or long periods of time sat by my computer doing nothing. Social media can also be a bit of a swine to play games with the mind if you're in a bad place: it can show you how happy and successful others are, when, in reality, you're only seeing the best bits of someone's life. Social media should come with a 'hazardous to one's health' warning on it. It can be a shallow, fake world.

Joe: Do you have any advice for authors combatting depression? Any tactics you use to stay positive or keep yourself distracted.

David: I've taken up kickboxing and started eating healthily. This, along with taking naps, has been working wonders! I've also cut my internet usage back and started leaving my phone at home when I go to work, take the family out or when I'm spending quality time with my wife or friends.

There have been blips along the way, but things have been 100% better. The moods and depressive bouts have been few and far between, and it's getting to a point where I'm starting to think I no longer need therapy. I've learned to lay a lot of my demons to bed.

So yeah, my advice would be plenty of exercise, good eating and get away from your computer every so often. Live life.

Joe: Have you ever experienced ignorance from publishers, editors or even readers regarding depression? Perhaps other authors?

David: No. In fact, I've found it to be the other way around. When I first spoke about having mental health issues on social media, there was an abundance of support—it was rather overwhelming! It helped, too. It's right when they say talking helps. It really does. Never be afraid to speak your mind, to tell those closest to you what's going on inside your head. Face your demons head on. Trust me, you'll feel so much better.

Joe: What advice do you want to give all the authors reading this book? Perhaps something you wish you'd done or learned early on in your career.

David: The only thing I regret is not seeking professional help for my mental health struggles sooner. It's held me back over the years, got in the way of my work and clouded my vision. Which, in turn, made me an angry, bitter person, and not just a depressive with anxiety issues.

If you know you have problems, go and get them solved—nothing will come of sitting on your hands. Believe me. I know how scary the thought of opening up is, about letting out all your nasty little demons, but it is so worth it. A huge weight will be removed.

The old cliché is right: a problem shared is a problem halved.

The Pessimistic Side of Horror

Luke Walker

Art is a mirror to society—or so they say. Writers or anyone working in the creative fields supposedly have a duty to hold that mirror up and reflect society's ills and ugliness right back in its face. If somebody wants to turn away from their reflection, well, that's their choice. Nobody is suggesting they're under any obligation to take a long look at that reflection.

Nobody but the writer who's watching the mirror begin to crack.

Of course, it's more than possible to simply write or create to entertain, and to do so without the slightest consideration of Saying Something Important. For what it's worth, this is how I work and if I had to boil down any writing advice to beginners, it would be *just tell your story and let the reader take whatever they want from it.* The chances are if you do want to get a view across, it'll come organically in the writing, anyway. Hold that mirror up, but don't shout about it. Let the reflection lurk in the background, peeking out from behind your characters and your plot. Let your characters tell their story as well as yours. Be subtle. Otherwise, you're in danger of alienating your reader because you're forcing your opinion on to them when they just came along for the ride of your tale.

Looking at your writing on a bigger scale and whatever your politics or personal beliefs, you'd have to be willingly blind to the state of the world right now. While it's never been anything other than a ridiculous mess run by the corrupt, the incompetent, the outright evil or stupid with enough decent people occasionally pulling us back from the brink, Planet Earth is in a bad way. Even without our petty squabbles over land and history and our rulers burying us in lie after lie to the point that the literal truth can be debated and picked apart, we're staring at the consequences of our damage to our home while we happily continue to cause more of that same damage. So, why the hell shouldn't writers—especially horror writers—hold up a mirror to our lives? The instant argument to that is why not elevate instead of deflate. After all, if everything is so utterly terrible, surely it's better to always strive to keep hope alive for readers who are more than likely looking to escape reality for the time it takes them to read a few hundred pages.

Surely that's better, right?

I don't know if it's better or right or wrong. I don't care in the least. I *do* care about it not being honest. Honesty is the cornerstone of the best writing as it is with all the creative arts. Genre is irrelevant with that issue. Your duty is to tell your story honestly.

For the horror writer, that can often mean digging deep into the muck and the grief of their own lives and saying *I see the world exactly how it is with its bleeding wounds and its fresh scars.* The world isn't pretty or fair or *nice.* Sure, it

97

has its moments. Those glorious occasions, usually so very brief, when you win. Those seconds and minutes are all the sweeter when they're least expected or they come when you've worked your fingers bloody for them. We all know what it is to spin the wheel and watch it hit. But the world doesn't care about our moments when it clicks into place, which is why we hold on to them with everything we have long after they become our past and live in memory.

Everybody knows this; it's the responsibility of you as a horror writer not to give a damn about the whole elevate or deflate angle. All you have to do with your work and your characters is tell the truth because we're adults. Readers know what to expect from the tropes in horror, and if they didn't want to run the risk of the writer showing them that the glass is most definitely half empty, they'd be reading something else entirely. Treat your readers like the grown-ups they are. Don't be afraid to push them down along with your characters. By all means, bring them back up for a time with a glimmer of the light at the end of the tunnel. That's how real-life works, after all. Even when we get dark, as in pitch-black, we can be saved at the last minute by something as relatively simple as a joke or a comment, by a friend or a loved one, by someone who knows us better than we know ourselves. They pull us up out of it. *You* as the writer have exactly the same power over your characters and therefore your readers. Know when to throw them a rope.

And know when to yank that rope away.

Obviously, going for the pessimistic side of writing, you run the real risk of depressing people. Worse, being preachy. Nobody wants a book to beat them over the head with a diatribe or non-stop negativity. Even if your readers believe our politicians are the best people for the job, that the environment isn't totally screwed and that the have-nots don't deserve any help, the chances are they'll see your writing as propaganda at worst or just plain amateur at best. The people who don't agree with your pessimism (or what you would probably rather call realism) won't appreciate you shoving it in their face so blatantly. As the kids no longer say, you need to keep it real. Take Stephen King's novel *Pet Sematary*. Probably his darkest work in terms of horror (spoilers incoming) and that horror is grounded in reality. Consider the principal plot points that set up the supernatural angle:

The Creeds move across country after buying a house (reality).

Louis Creed is a doctor starting a new job (reality).

They become friendly with their neighbour (reality).

They learn the history of their neighbourhood, especially the background to a certain woodland area with markers and graves built by young hands (reality).

All areas we're familiar with because more or less everyone knows about jobs and neighbours and homes. Then the book gets as dark as midnight and we know about that, too. We know loss and grief and our good lives being dropped headfirst into hell without a second's warning. Pessimistic? Certainly, particularly the ending of the novel. Truthful? Definitely. The key issue is that King keeps the pessimism and the bleakness rooted in the world of real things. We *know* it's all going to end horribly; we're neck deep in the same hell as the Creeds. Of course, we can walk away after we've finished King's bleakest tale. Lucky us.

As dark as *Pet Sematary* is, King doesn't drown us with negativity and cynicism. We're already in the journey with the Creeds and we came willingly as your readers do and will. Let them see the negatives fully with the positives in reach. Just.

That isn't to say you have to go straight for the downer angle with every story you tell or stick to a *kill em all* ending because that's the sole facet of horror some people are willing to consider. Yes, you'll need to get down in the dirt if you're writing in this genre; you'll also need to decide on your scale (and possible limits) of violence. Bear in mind, violence is a lot more than cutting off heads, stabbing your characters in the eyes or filling them full of bullet holes. Mental horror, emotional torture and the destruction of the tiny hope that is keeping your character alive when everything is falling apart...*that's* violence. And as with your personal limits and requirements on the gore, you need to decide on the levels of the emotional brutality you want to write about as well as how much you want to put your readers through. It's easy to just cut loose, go nuts and think *I'm a horror writer, so I need to give them all hell.* At the same time, you need to know when to step back and hint at what's coming...or what's hiding around the corner on the next page.

Case in point—years back, I read a nasty horror which opened with the detailed torture and murder of a couple in their home. And I mean, *nasty.* The problem was the reader didn't have the slightest chance to get to know the characters before the violence. They were simply place-holders for pain. Even one or two scenes to set them up as flesh and blood (before all the actual blood) would have been a big help. Physical violence and gore are tools at your disposal. Know when to use them or when to put them back in the box and reach for something a little more subtle. You're in the business of being truthful and of showing (not telling) your readers that your fiction is every bit as bloody and agonising as the news; at the same time, you need that physicality to be as effective as possible. Take the character out of your story as well as from the people in the story and you'll either numb your reader or outright depress them.

Finally, you need to consider your ending, its power and its impact. With that, you must bear in mind the world beyond the story. It's the world outside the reader's focus on your words. As I write this in early August of 2019, the news is full of yet more mass shootings in America (and by the time this is published, there will have been others. Far too many others); Britain has its third leader in as many years with absolutely no indication that the government will admit Brexit is an economic and national disaster; politics has divided friends, families and entire countries along vehement, ugly lines, and we've turned the planet into a ticking ecological bomb. Grim thoughts, right? While there will hopefully always be people striving to stop us all from jumping off into the abyss, you have to always remember you are telling the truth. We're in trouble—*all of us.* And it will take something pretty spectacular from our leaders as well as from the people who feel utterly powerless to save the day. The ending of your story can be edging towards restoring the natural balance of your characters' lives (I'd be surprised if in any horror novel that the people who make it to the end are untouched; I'd consider you a liar if you force a happy ending and everything is fine), but the chances are your characters will be physically, emotionally and mentally marked by what you've put them through. Good. So they should. And so should your readers. *Marked* is simply a nicer way of saying *scarred.* I don't mean you have to be a brutal monster with your denouement; I don't mean you should find your readers' triggers and mercilessly hammer on them (trigger warnings are another subject, one which I'd advise you to research and form your own view regarding their necessity). What I do mean is don't be afraid to go dark for the ending of your story. Everything outside your words and pages is dark; why shouldn't your writing be the same? You and I are not in the business of holding our readers' hands and as I said earlier, they're adults. They should know what they're putting themselves in for when they start your book—the very real risk of the guy not saving the girl, of the zombies chewing on the hero's brain in the last scene, of you merrily vomiting a bloodbath on the page as the story comes to its natural conclusion.

Of the good guys losing and losing *hard*.

Of course, it's possible for there to be something approaching a downer ending in almost every genre. However, horror is probably the only one in which it's more than acceptable. It's often expected. Films are probably more open to this than literature. Think of how many horror movies you've seen which feature a final jump scare to suggest (or outright state) the killer is still alive, the vengeful spirit hasn't been exorcised or that the slimy thing in the basement is waiting for a new family to move into the house. Actually, you'd be better off thinking of the films that *don't* feature that kind of ending. It'd be a shorter list and save you a lot of time. Obviously, films and books are entirely different mediums. Horror films are often set up for the inevitable sequels while it's generally considered more preferable for a book to have a sense of closure with maybe a hint the story could continue. How open-ended you want to leave your book is up to you, the publisher and, most importantly, the story. If forcing the idea of a follow-up grates against the closure, don't do it. If there is natural space for your monster to return, then by all means keep the door open for them. Even if it's just enough for them to slide their claws through.

Ultimately, you have to decide on your ending and if a downer is the right route to take. If you outline your plot and rigorously stick to that outline, the chances are you'll know before you write the first word who will survive and what will be left of them. Wing the story and your ending can be as much of a surprise to you as it is to the reader. Personally, I usually work with a loose outline with a vague idea of the outcome although I'm more than happy for that conclusion to change before I reach it. After all, none of us know when our own outcome will hit us. And we sure as hell don't know the final result of our confused and hurting world. As the writer, it's your responsibility to ensure your ending is every bit as truthful as the rest of the book. Don't be afraid to consider the prospect of evil triumphing and your good guys losing everything for one simple reason.

We're in trouble. All of us. And you're showing your readers that unless we keep fighting evil in whatever form it chooses to take, then your pessimism is justified.

And the mirror you're holding up to reality is starting to crack.

Women and Violence: The Evolution of the Final Girl

Stephanie M. Wytovich

In 1992, Carol Clover coined the term "Final Girl" in her book *Men, Women, and Chainsaws: Gender in the Modern Horror Film.* Since then, the concept of the last surviving female—complete with her virginity, a strict moral system, and more often than not, a rocking hot body—has been seen time and time again in horror films, most notably so in slashers, but in contemporary film and media, it's now a concept that is being challenged and reinterpreted for its impossible standards, image, and dedication to the male gaze. Long gone are the days of women being pigeonholed into a role riddled with stereotypes and consequences due to a heaping fear of all things feminine. Instead, we're moving into an era of story lines and character arcs where the woman truly can have it all, and most importantly, not be punished for it.

But first things first: who *is* a Final Girl? If you've watched any number of horror films, she's fairly easy to pick out, and not just because she's usually the protagonist of the story. Our girl is typically shy, book smart, not terribly into her looks or fashion, and she exudes an air of innocence. Maybe she has a boyfriend, and maybe she doesn't, but she's definitely still a virgin, and the idea of sex might even seem foreign or disgusting to her. She's also typically the girl who isn't afraid to separate herself from the crowd based on a gut instinct or perhaps even a heightened sense of right or wrong, and when push comes to shove, she's a fighter, a survivor, and sometimes that's due to a past event, family history, or her own personal trauma, and other times, it's because her naivety makes her the bigger prize for the killer. Clover writes:

> The image of the distressed female most likely to linger in memory is the image of the one who did not die: the survivor, or Final Girl. She is the one who encounters the mutilated bodies of her friends and perceives the full extent of the preceding horror and of her own peril; who is chased, cornered, wounded; whom we see scream, stagger, fall, rise, and scream again. She is abject terror personified. If her friends knew they were about to die only seconds before the event, the Final Girl lives with the knowledge for long minutes or hours. She alone looks death in the face, but she alone also finds the strength either to stay the killer long enough to be rescued (ending A) or to kill him herself (ending B). But in either case, from 1974 on, the survivor figure has been female. (39)

Yet beyond the façade of a girl whose charm and gullibility alone makes us want to root for her, she's also a character who's still, at heart, developed for the male gaze. She might find the bodies and go head-to-head with the killer in the end, but she remains a culmination of someone who is strong, but not *too* strong, and pretty, but not *too* pretty. Essentially, she's chaste enough not to be punished, but not threatening enough that men feel emasculated by cheering her on. It's a fine line to walk when you're a Final Girl, but at the end of the movie, not matter how high your body count is, or how many times you were able to outsmart the villain, the Final Girl remains a figure cast in the light of independence while still being confined by patriarchal ideals and fantasies surrounding the female form.

From a sociological perspective, the contradiction of the Final Girl makes sense. Women wanted (and want) to have autonomy over their lives, but were feeling the pressure from conservative dogma surrounding a woman's place domestically and in the workplace, and then with how she conducts herself both privately and in public. During the horror boom of the 70s and 80s, women continued to fight for equality and control of their own bodies. Second-wave feminist ideology emerged during the 1960s and carried on well into the 80s. This was a time when women publicly talked about and demanded action over issues concerning, but not limited to: domestic violence, marital rape, and reproductive rights. When we take this into consideration and look at how this translates into the horror genre, we see two types of exaggerated female characters: (1) the oversexualized, undereducated, oftentimes blonde bimbo who dies tragically, graphically, and usually while naked or on display due to her promiscuous nature, and (2) the innocent bookworm who has a healthy fear and cautious nature toward all things strange and unusual and who is definitely 100% a virgin. At first glance, this is problematic because it's characterizing women into one of two choices, both of which are extreme in their nature. At second glace, we can see a split politically in regard to liberal and conservative inclinations toward the female body; one is more accepting of sex, multiple partners, control over one's own body, whereas the other is more refined, covered up, and perhaps even more faith-oriented when it comes to their core beliefs about sex. As such, the Final Girl—the latter of the two—becomes a model for how women should act because she is the one who rises up and survives the carnage due to conforming to society's preconceived notions toward how a woman should act, while her counterpoint is a cautionary tale, a warning to all women who dare not play by the rules and who exploit themselves or give in to their desires. That's why Randy from Wes Craven's 1996 movie *Scream* goes on a tangent about the rules of surviving horror films and why they continue to echo inside us today. Randy states:

> First, you can never have sex. Second, you can never drink or do drugs. Big no no. It's a sin. It's an extension of number one. And last, you can never, ever, ever under any circumstances say "I'll be right back," cause you won't be back. (Craven)

What's ironic about this is that when we talk about *cardinal rules* and *sins* in the horror genre, we as voyeurs to the violence and sexual nature of these films are both putting into place and solidifying the religious connotations and punishments that Randy is—tongue-in-cheek—making fun of. We expect, and delight in, the moment when a character starts to party, or when she takes off her shirt, because we know what's going to happen next. We know that her death is a steppingstone to the Final Girl's inevitable victory, and we cheer for her bloodshed because *she deserves it*. She reached too high, she wanted too much, she gave into her urges, spread her legs…

Hell, it's almost like she wanted to be able to make her own decisions based on what she wanted to do and what made her feel comfortable and happy.

You can see my point now then, yes?

But the archetype of the Final Girl isn't all bad. With her, women are still seeing themselves succeed over trials and tribulations due to perseverance, strength, intelligence, and determination. We're oftentimes seeing the woman close out the film with a final castration scene—sorry Freud!—where she is the one penetrating the villain via a weapon, usually a knife, thereby taking back her power as she refuses to be another victim. It's illuminating and inspiring to see a woman walking away from the flames because for so long in the media, women have been the body count, the damsel-in-distress. What's truly great about the Final Girl is that she doesn't need to be saved; she can, and will, do it herself.

A classic example of this is one of my favorite Final Girls: Sidney Prescott. When *Scream* first debuted, Sidney quickly joined the ranks of other notable Final Girls such as Laurie Strode (*Halloween,* 1978*)* and Nancy Thompson (*A Nightmare on Elm Street*, 1984). She was the clean-cut, virginal brunette who was traumatized due to her mother's murder and who was being constantly pressured by her friends and boyfriend to get over herself, to start having fun, and most importantly, to start having sex.

Throughout the series, Sidney's character is one of strength, intellect, and courage, and much like how her predecessors tackled Michael Myers and Freddy Krueger, she didn't run from Ghostface or his incessant need to stab at her. Ghostface's sexual frustration and obsession aside, Sidney learned to cope with her fears, overcome her trauma, and refuse the label of victim even when her life is consistently turned upside down. But even with all of that, Sidney is bound by the rules, and when she has sex, she's attacked for it. When she dates, her boyfriends tend to die. Even her mother, Maureen—who was described as a bit of a harlot—was murdered for her promiscuity.

Case in point: good girls survive, and bad girls don't.

However, times changing and with it, so is the appearance of and definition of the Final Girl. These days, women are writing the playbook, and admittedly as a female, the voyeurism that's being experienced is transformed, too. Instead of cheering on the monster as he goes to punish teenagers for their lack of decorum, I'm now cheering on the girl as she becomes more and more confident with who she is and who she was meant to be, which sometimes is a hero and other times borders the monstrous itself. These girls aren't ashamed that they bleed, or that they're sexual beings, and they certainly aren't being controlled by anyone other than themselves. One of my favorite examples of this shift in gender stereotyping is Robert Eggers' 2015 film, *The VVitch*.

Here the audience is introduced to Thomasin, a young adolescent girl who has been forced to leave her previous home alongside her family due to some type of undisclosed conflict they had with the rest of the village. As part of a devout Puritan family, her life in their new home consists primarily of domestic duties and prayer, but when her baby brother Samuel goes missing under her watch, speculation as to her motives and true identity start to arise. It's not long after that the word "witch" begins to be thrown around, and as each member of her family turns their accusations toward her, Thomasin is forced to both protect herself and as a result, question her identity.

One of the many inspiring facets of this film is that Thomasin's character revels in the beauty and bounty of choice. She is believed to be a witch and therefore is seen as a concubine of the devil, an evil seductress. Her family tells her over and over again that she is this vile thing, and no matter how many times she begs and pleads with them, no matter how many times she denies it and recites the Lord's prayer, she as a budding, blossoming woman complete with her first blood, is shunned, attacked, and persecuted against. However, it's the end of the film, the moment after Thomasin's family is dead that she, the Final Girl covered in blood and victory, makes a choice.

Thomasin chooses to both seek out and sign the Devil's book, to disrobe and walk naked in the moonlight, to fly toward her freedom and independence from the patriarchy and the church, the very life she'd been longing for but was constantly denied by her family. She leaves behind her old self as she walks into the woods as a fierce, dangerous, sexually confident woman, yet it's the acceptance of this so-called monstrous side that allows her to be free, to be safe, and to be happy.

In *The VVitch,* Thomasin takes back her power by making an unpopular choice and sticking to it. She saves herself when the world and everyone in it turned away from her, and she both protected and gained control of her body while giving in to what she desired most: freedom. It's enlightening, empowering, and most importantly, it's rife with acceptance. It gives women the chance to be desirable and to desire, while also telling them that their choices about what to wear, how to act, and when to speak don't make them deserving of or blameful for any sort of violence or violent acts that happen to them. Much like how second-wave feminism affected the interpretation of the Final Girl in the 70s and 80s, third and fourth-wave feminism—with a heavy focus on assault, rape culture, and the Me Too Movement—encourages this current shift in one of horror's most beloved archetypes. This reversal of the stereotype is important because it shirks off any preconceived notions of expectations, thereby making the character arc unpredictable, fresh, and filled with possibility.

After all, there isn't only one way to be a woman.

So why should there be a formula for a Final Girl?

Works Cited:
Clover, Carol. *Men, Women, and Chainsaws: Gender in the Modern Horror Film.* Princeton, Princeton University Press, 1992.
Craven, Wes, director. *Scream.* Dimension Films, 1996.

Work Consulted:
Eggers, Robert, director. *The VVitch.* A24, 2015.

The Importance of Setting

Marie O'Regan

When you think of a horror story, where do you imagine it taking place? That might seem a strange question, but everyone's definition of horror is different. By no means are ghosts and demons the full extent of the subject. To some the word horror evokes cemeteries at night—things capering behind the headstones, ghostly visitations…you get the idea. To others, the word horror evokes the slaughter of innocents by a serial killer in the relatively humdrum world of the everyday, the descent (gradual or otherwise) into madness, or a child abducted by person or persons (or *things*) unknown. It's all relative, in other words. Horror means very different things to very different people, but for our purposes can be reduced to one element: the emotion invoked when reading a piece of horror fiction or watching a horror movie.

There are varying degrees of that emotion, of course—dread, shock, terror...all engendered by reactions to something that frightens you, perhaps disgusts you, or just makes you look over your shoulder, searching for the reason the hairs at the nape of your neck are prickling. But the common denominator is always fear.

Used effectively, the setting of your story can really crank this up. It can become almost another character—with its own personality and tone, supporting and enhancing the emotional reaction you're seeking to elicit from your reader. Your use of similes, adjectives, the way you describe the scene, all have an effect on setting the tone of your story. Just having the protagonist descend into a 'dark, clammy cellar—the sound of water dripping echoing somewhere close, unseen—isn't enough. No, it's not exactly a warm, comforting scenario, but how about adding some dialogue: '"Hello?" the child's voice crept up the stairs towards me, quavering in its attempt to be brave. "Mister? Can you hear me? Can't you see me? I'm right here..." Her voice faded away at the last, until it was no more than a whisper borne on the blast of cold air that hit me... Was a window broken somewhere? I cast the beam from the torch around this cell-like space, to no avail. Wherever she was, she was long gone from here.'

You've set the scene for a pretty creepy situation, which seems to be leaning towards a ghost story, but you never can tell. The child could be something other than a child, and perhaps laying in wait...or there really could be a child hiding, from some sinister third character, either living or dead. The possibilities are endless, but definitely influenced by the surroundings.

Some of the most famous genre novels and short stories are heavily dependent on their setting for atmosphere—the two go hand in hand. *Salem's Lot*, by Stephen King; *The Fog* by James Herbert; the well-known short story *The*

Yellow Wallpaper, by Charlotte Perkins Gilman…all are excellent examples of this. King's vampire novel postulates what would happen if the vampire of old legends came to small-town America, and he paints a vivid picture of the banality of everyday life there, together with the inhabitants' initial inability to process facts so far out of their experience. Herbert's novel is set in the everyday world, but all the violence and horror in the novel arises out of exposure to the eponymous fog, changing people's behaviour in an instant—turning them into human monsters. Gilman's short story is a masterpiece of atmosphere, gradually insinuating a growing terror into a prosaic tale of a sickly woman (her illness is never specified, merely described as 'nervous weakness') resting in a room that was long ago decorated with a wallpaper she really hates. Slowly, she comes to believe it contains the root of all her ills.

"At night in any kind of light, in twilight, candlelight, lamplight, and worst of all by moonlight, it becomes bars! The outside pattern I mean, and the woman behind it is as plain as can be."

For most of the story the reader is convinced the woman is imagining things, but gradually her fancies seem more plausible, the behaviour of her husband and sister-in-law more sinister, so that by the end of the story all appears very real, leading to a riveting dénouement. Gilman herself suffered from depression and this story vividly details the 'rest cure' she was forced to take, to little effect—although it did at least provide the inspiration for this haunting tale of paranoia. It is the very normality of the setting that makes the story so frightening, involving as it does either 'ghosts' trying to get out of the wallpaper, or a woman slowly but surely going insane.

There are no real rules for where to set your horror novel (or film), but the more prosaic and mundane the setting, the greater the capacity to make you—as reader or viewer—fearful. It is far more unsettling to wonder what's making that scuffling noise behind the washing machine than it is to enter a new environment—whether that's a new school, or a world reached through the opening of a puzzle box. To use a film example, think of the film *White Noise*. It starts out as the story of a man who loses his wife, ostensibly to an accident. It takes a twist into scarier territory when he hears her voice in static on the radio, and others crowd in, eager for their voices to be heard. Suddenly everyday objects such as the TV, radio…even reflections in glass, become infinitely more threatening. He starts to search for his wife, to talk to her one more time, maybe find out how she really died—and his search leads him to the realisation that he can sometimes tune into people *before* they die, and perhaps even prevent their deaths. Naturally, there is a force that wants to stop him.

In films such as those of the Saw franchise, or Scream, there is no supernatural element—the dread arises from watching the protagonist(s) struggling to survive the predations of an unknown, though all-too-human, assailant. The settings are those of the everyday. In the case of the first *Saw* film, just one room—a 'public' bathroom—with two men chained and forced to try and solve a puzzle. In the case of *Scream*, a young girl is chased through the high school and her home by an unknown attacker. The very ordinariness of the setting heightens the tension—we are aware that this could happen to any of us, in one form or another.

So look around with you with newly opened eyes, and imagine what the most effective setting for your horror tale might be.

A Tear in the Fabric of the Cosmos:
The Importance of Algernon Blackwood's *The Willows*?

Jasper Bark

It's my belief that *The Willows* is, without doubt, one of the most important works of 20th Century Horror. In order to explain why this is such an important work, I'm going to have to discuss a few minor spoilers or, at least, take away some of the surprise in discovering the story for yourself.

If you haven't read the story yet, I suggest you stop reading at the end of this paragraph and go grab a copy of the novella. Crystal Lake Publishing has just released a fabulous new edition that I can recommend. It's also online and in any number of anthologies, so quick, go grab a copy. It's going to be a wild ride down the Danube (and that's the only spoiler, I'll allow).

***

Okay, you're back. It was great wasn't it, and aren't you glad you saved reading this until you'd read it? Now, let's discuss what makes *The Willows* so important to the horror genre.

The Willows first appeared in 1907 in Blackwood's second collection: *The Listener and Other Stories*. It was probably written sometime in 1906 and was based on two canoeing trips Blackwood took along the Danube in 1900 and 1901, with Wilfred Wilson, upon whom many believe the character of the 'Swede' is based.

Genre fiction is more autobiographical than you might think, the apparent distance imaginative stories give the author, means they often let way more of themselves slip than they might realise. Commentators believe much of Blackwood's fiction is inspired by events from his own life. *The Willows* is one of three stories from the collection that are thought to have drawn on Blackwood's personal experience (the other two being *The Listener* and *The Old Man of Visions*).

So, it's very possible that Blackwood and Wilson did find themselves camped out on an island in the Danube, once filled with willow bushes, and now lost to floods. What's more, Blackwood had been fascinated with the esoteric since his childhood, when a family friend left a book on Hinduism at his parents' house. As an adult, he joined the Hermetic Order of the Golden Dawn (along with his contemporaries Aleister Crowley and Arthur Machen) and dabbled in occult matters. He might even have had direct experiences that inspired the supernatural elements of this tale. It's interesting to note that, unlike Lovecraft—who so admired Blackwood—and, in fact, a sizeable majority of horror writers, Blackwood actually believed in the supernatural.

For me, what makes *The Willows* such an important story is that it acts as a bridge between the weird tales that had gone before and the horror fiction that was to come. The language and pace of the novella are in keeping with

Victorian fiction. The fact that the narrator remains unnamed, and his companion is referred to simply as 'the Swede,' follows the conventions of 19th rather than 20th Century fiction. Our protagonists' expedition down the Danube is also dealt with in an antiquated fashion. Modern fiction would offer at least some motivation for making the trip and provide a little backstory. Blackwood presents it as something of a 'ripping wheeze,' the Danube is there, the two men have a canoe, and that's explanation enough for their jaunt.

Then there's the matter of two men, who are emotionally attached, spending so much time alone, in an isolated setting, that requires physical intimacy. This probably wouldn't have raised any eyebrows when it was published. However, these days, as a bi-sexual man, I can't help projecting my own subtext onto the situation. A subtext that modern authors, like Clive Barker (in *In the Hills, the Cities*) and Laird Baron (in *Mysterium Tremendum*) make refreshingly explicit when depicting similar situations.

While these elements tie the story to the past, there are many more that look to the future. Prime among these is setting. Up to this point, weird fiction had relied heavily on the Victorian ghost story and gothic novels by the likes of Horace Walpole and Ann Radcliffe. Most of these were primarily set in ancient castles, large country houses, or other enclosed spaces. Blackwood, conversely, excelled in depictions of the outdoors.

The Willows starts with a widescreen description of the river's course and our focus slowly pushes in to a close up of the terrain, until we find ourselves trapped on a diminishing island, populated by willows. A warning from a Hungarian officer, about becoming stranded if the river subsides, establishes the setting as extremely hazardous, but, by the climax, the physical dangers of the island become mere symbols for perils that make death at the hands of the elements seem merciful.

Fritz Leiber, Richard Matheson and Ramsey Campbell helped establish the modern horror story by taking the action out of haunted mansions and graveyards and placing it in contemporary settings in broad daylight. *The Willows* pre-empts this innovation by some thirty to forty years.

Under the influence of writers like Charles L. Grant, horror writers from the late seventies onwards, placed an increasing emphasis on the importance of atmosphere in the horror story. If *The Willows* is distinguished by one single feature, it would be the atmosphere of mounting dread Blackwood manages to conjure up. To such a degree it might be considered an object lesson in creating atmosphere.

Another theme that has become increasingly prevalent in modern horror is the cosmic threat posed by a hostile universe in which the human race is nothing more than an infinitesimal irrelevance. Generally known as 'cosmic horror,' it's often traced back to H. P. Lovecraft but, as we've previously noted, Lovecraft was a huge admirer of Blackwood's work and was highly influenced by it. *The Willows* was his favourite story. In *Supernatural Horror in Literature*, Lovecraft acknowledges this influence, professing that: "an impression of lasting poignancy is produced without a single strained passage or a single false note." While I admire Lovecraft's work tremendously, I have to say that I find his cosmic creatures, which are really just ancient and immense extra-terrestrials, to be far less frightening than Blackwood's numinous beings from a wholly different dimension.

Finally, what makes the story especially chilling, for me, is the way Blackwood delineates the psychological deterioration of the two protagonists. Once again this is a good four decades before Robert Bloch, and others, turned from capes and fangs to the works of Freud to create what we now know as psychological horror.

The Willows is both of its time and ahead of it. It contains the seeds of every direction the horror genre would take over the next hundred years. This gives it a timeless quality that never fails to enthral, no matter how many times you've read it. It doesn't just chill you, it leaves you with a feeling of genuine awe and the lingering sense that the fabric of the cosmos has been torn and you've been given a brief glimpse of what lies beyond.

An Interview with Tim Waggoner

Joe Mynhardt

Joe Mynhardt: Let's start off with the horror genre itself. What makes it so appealing for so many of us? And even more so why in the written format?

Tim Waggoner: Horror stories allow us to confront our deepest fears through the buffer of fiction. Wrestling with the darkest questions of human existence–why is there violence, pain, cruelty, and death?–can be emotionally overwhelming. These questions can be too intense to deal with directly. Like an eclipse, the only way to safely view these aspects of life is indirectly. Horror allows us to do this. Horror can serve as a buffer in another way. It can distract us from the horrors of the real world, all of which are far more terrifying than any story about a ghost or vampire. Horror writers are like dark clowns that caper in front of our readers, making grotesque faces in the hope that the audience won't look over our shoulder and see the true darkness of existence behind us. Horror also allows us to exercise our imagination in ways other genres can't. The Dark is a blank canvas upon which our imaginations can paint. Anything could be lurking in the shadows...anything at all.

In visual media, horror stories are fully realized and presented to the audience to passively consume. In the written form, authors give readers the tools to tell themselves a story. The reader is an active participant. The story is fully realized only in the reader's mind, making it a far more intimate process than watching a film or TV show or playing a videogame. With written stories, the horror happens *inside* us, giving the written form far more power than the visual form.

Joe: Just so you know, some of the best advice for authors I've ever read come from your articles. So what, in your expert opinion should an author, who after the initial excitement of starting their career or a new project for that matter, do when the excitement withers and is replaced by self-doubt?

Tim: Forget yourself and focus on the writing. Easy to say, but not so easy to do, of course. But after writing fiction for close to forty years now, it's the only solution I've found that works. Self-doubt has the word *self* in it, after all. When we're overly conscious of ourselves as writers trying to craft a story, we can get in our own way. It's like when you become overly aware of a simple action you do every day–like walking–and you suddenly feel awkward and uncomfortable doing it. You inevitably end up stumbling. As writers, what we're trying to produce are stories that satisfy an audience. And that's where our salvation lies. When in doubt, focus on the next word of a story, and then the word after that, and the word after that. Don't ask yourself if these words are any good. The question is meaningless when you draft. The only thing that produces writing is writing, so we write. We need to try to stay the hell out of our own way and let the words do their thing. And if the story that ultimately results is never published, so what? We created it, we learned something from doing so, and it's time to move on and write something else. It's the artistic version of Newton's First Law: An object at rest tends to stay at rest, an object in motion tends to stay in motion. Writing is how we keep moving, and as long as you're moving, there's less time for self-doubt.

Joe: What are your thoughts on the psyche of a horror writer? What makes them (us) such unique human beings?

Tim: Several years ago, I attended a conference in Minneapolis with the chair of my department. (I'm an English professor in my day job.) One day we explored the city for a few hours, and when we returned to the hotel, we sat down in the lobby, and my chair–who was a literary poet–asked me why I wrote horror. I thought for a moment, and I asked him if he'd seen the banana on the sidewalk that we'd passed multiple times during our exploration of the city. He had no idea what I was talking about. I told him that not only did I see the banana every time we walked by it, I could tell him the state it was in each time. The first time it was a whole, untouched banana, but by the last time we encountered it, it was flattened brown mush smeared on the pavement. "That's why I write horror," I told him. "I see the squashed bananas."

Horror writers are fascinated with deviations from the norm–small ones, large ones, it doesn't matter. Our imaginations seize on these details and we wonder what the story is behind them. These deviations are signals to our minds: something isn't right here, and we become instantly more alert. We sense possible danger (even if it's only mild) and our minds start racing. I've read articles in which psychologists suggest that reading and watching horror allow people to develop stronger survival skills. We engage in fictional scenarios to explore what we would do in dangerous situations. Horror writers see the squashed bananas of existence, and we process our feelings about them through our work. Plus, writing scary stories is a hell of a lot of fun!

Joe: Which aspect(s) of writing (voice, characterization, setting, mood, show vs. tell, dialogue etc.) would you place the most importance on and why? An aspect all young authors should start working on, and which all authors should continue to develop. Or is it all just a balancing act?

Tim: It is a balancing act, but if I had to choose one aspect that's most vital, I'd choose immersive point of view. Almost all of us, no matter how much we read, have taken in thousands upon thousands of hours of visual media. As I said earlier about the effectiveness of written horror, visual media demands very little of us. We sit passively while the media feeds us all the information we need. The action in our visual media–at least in their current form–consist primarily of sound and movement. The appearance of things–the setting, the characters, the background–is created instantly by the picture we're presented with. It comes to us as a unified whole, but writers can only create our effects one word at a time. So when someone raised on a steady diet of visual media sits down to write fiction, they write from a distant point of view, as if they're a passive audience member watching events play out on a screen, and they only depict sound and movement, forgetting any other types of details. And since our visual media doesn't create information word by word, beginners are generally terrible at description. Writing with an immersive point of view—writing as if you are living inside the character's head and thinking, feeling, seeing, hearing, smelling, tasting, touching, and doing everything that he or she is—makes your fiction involving. You create a reality for the reading through a character's perceptions. You depict life the way we all live it, as a multitude of information coming into our minds through our sensory organs and stimulating reactions from us. Plus, an immersive point of view is an experience that, so far, our visual media can't create. It's the prime feature that fiction has to offer that nothing else can.

So many other problems can be addressed through an immersive point of view. It helps develop character, helps you decide what to describe based on what the character would pay attention to at any moment, it helps you orient your reader in the setting because the character is clearly oriented in the setting, and so on.

Joe: As a former educator, I understand all too well the importance of dissecting and studying a problem or obstacle, but how should an author find the balance between letting their creative minds free and treating the writing craft as a science to be studied.

Tim: Writers can take classes, read how-to-write books, watch instructional videos on YouTube, and listen to writers give advice on panels at conferences. But there are only two real ways to become a writer: read a lot and write a lot. The act of reading with conscious awareness of what makes a story work for you and what doesn't helps you study the nuts and bolts of composing fiction from the outside, and then the writing of stories helps you study the creation of fiction from the inside. Creativity is always inherent in these two aspects of becoming a writer, since you're regularly experiencing others' art and producing your own. But creativity truly blossoms when you've read and written so much that you stop consciously thinking about the basics. The awareness of craft is still there, but it's become internalized, such an integral part of you that you're not really aware of it, or at least you don't practice it self-consciously. It's like sports. When you're first learning a sport, you have to work on conditioning your body, developing muscle memory, internalizing all the rules and moves. But once you become experienced, your conscious mind isn't focused on the basics anymore. You just do them, freeing your mind to perform at a higher level. This level is when writers—or any artists—reach a point where their mastery of craft allows them to fully express their creativity. The initial stage of a writer's journey is more about studying and solving problems consciously, while the later stage is more about developing and exercising the intuitive creativity necessary for artistic expression.

I'm honestly not sure how writers move between these stages. I've taught and mentored many writers who never progress beyond the beginning stage. They continue to look outside themselves to improve their writing, never reaching the point where they're able to look inside. Then there are the writers who begin by looking inside themselves and never progress to looking outside. One type learns craft but not expression, the other learns expression but not craft. The writers who become professionals are those who progress through both stages until craft and expression are operating simultaneously and continuously. If I were to express this as a formula, it would go something like this: Learning Craft →Developing Expression →Exercising both Craft and Expression Fully and Simultaneously. My guess is that professional writers spend most of their careers in the third stage, either satisfied where they're at or constantly striving to evolve further. But I have no idea how to help someone move through the stages. Maybe it's a natural progression that can be assisted somewhat, but not taught. I don't know. I'll have to think about this!

Podcast for Promotion

Armand Rosamilia

Not only have I been podcasting for the past six years, I've taken advantage of being a guest on other podcasts to help raise awareness for my work. Plus it's a lot of fun.

I'm going to (mostly) focus on the guest aspect, and how you can use it to get the word out about your latest and greatest release. Lucky for you there are quite a few great podcasts that will be a great fit for you no matter the genre or subgenre of your work.

A few things when you're searching and ultimately doing some podcast interviews:

Have something to promote. If your newest book is a year old, maybe get a list of podcasts to be interviewed on in the future…like, when the next book is coming out or is live. Listeners will want to go out and buy the new book you've been talking about for the last hour. If it's not even available as a pre-order...they'll forget about it. Timing is everything. Having the product ready to be purchased is why you're doing the interviews.

Timing really is everything. Most podcasts I've ever been interviewed on run about two or three weeks ahead, so being interviewed today doesn't necessarily mean it will go live until a couple of weeks later. If your book is already live and *now* you're starting to do interviews, you're already a few weeks behind. Most of the time, if I'm doing an interview for a future release, I'll let the host know ahead of time when my book is going live. They'll usually be cool and adjust to get your interview in and the interview live to coincide.

Research the podcast. Is it one that interviews guests, and those guests happen to write in your genre? If you see a lot of your peers being interviewed on the podcast, listen to the episodes. Heck, listen to all the episodes of the podcast regardless of the guest to hear if you'd be a good fit. I was once on a podcast that I hadn't listened to before going on, basing it on the previous guests. The co-host spent the hour making fart noises whenever I spoke, and it was so unprofessional I would never go back on no matter what. I could've saved myself some time and energy by listening to the previous episodes before agreeing to go on. I never made that mistake again, either.

Don't be on-time. Show up a few minutes early. Just because the podcaster has invited you to be interviewed at nine in the morning, showing up right on the dot is rude, to be blunt. Act like you're headed to a job interview. Do you walk into the office right at nine and expect your future boss to be impressed with you? Often, podcasters have lined up a few guests that day for future episodes. They'd really love to have the sound and everything perfect before they start actually interviewing you. A few minutes ahead of time is all they're asking. Even if they're running late or get on right at the moment, it's their show. Their rules. The way they operate. At least you'll be ready.

The right environment to be interviewed. Is that your dog barking in the background or the kids singing along to the YouTube video on an endless loop? To be a great guest you don't need your own recording studio, but you need quiet. With today's recording equipment, it's easier than ever to get a quality interview down...but the podcaster needs your help.

If you're going to use your phone to be interviewed, find a quiet spot. Sit in a closet. Stay out of the bathroom with the echo. Don't pace around the house so the noises come and go. Standing outside means birds and airplanes and the weird kid down the street singing Britney Spears songs while revving his dirt bike.

Ideally, a decent microphone and a pair of headphones on your end will work wonders.

Listen to the question. I can't tell you how many times I've asked a question to a guest and they've either ignored it or twisted it to get to the point they wanted to make right in the beginning of the interview. They're so excited to talk about their new book or something they find interesting, they jump right in.

I've had the pleasure of being interviewed on podcasts where the interviewer has a conversation with you, and the questions flow out of that organically. It becomes less an interview and more like two buddies hanging out and talking about their passion for writing.

The interviewer might have a set of questions in front of him, so be aware there might be a specific format they want to run the interview with. Be aware and roll with it.

Cheat sheet. If you know you want to get in specific information about your latest release, jot down some notes on an index card. I try to have three facts ready to go in case the interview lags or I see a natural opening to toss one in and let it lead to further questions.

After each interview, throw it away. If you're going to do multiple interviews, especially all in a short span of time, you want it to seem fresh. The worst thing is to do the same basic interview over and over. It gets boring for you and for the listeners.

Change up your answers. I'm not saying you lie, telling the podcaster in one interview you're a game warden in your normal life and then switch it up and talk about being an astronaut in the next. Based on previous episodes (which you've researched before, right?) you can focus on different aspects of your life or work or whatever in a subtle way based on the podcaster's interests and questions to former guests, so listeners who have already heard you on a previous podcast can find something different and interesting about you and your book.

Ask how long the interview will be. This will help you get your points across in a timely manner and make for a more organic interview. If the interview will only run about ten minutes as a segment, make sure you're front-loading your information about your book so you don't miss anything. If it will go an hour, take your time. Ease into it. Show your personality and have some fun. You'll get a better understanding of the pacing thanks to listening to previous interviews, too.

You're not selling your book. You're selling you. Remember that. Yes, your newest book is what you want the listeners to buy, but they don't want to part with their hard-earned money unless they see a need. Half the battle of selling books is by being funny, interesting and knowledgeable. Not about the book itself, but about you. A fun interaction between you and the host goes a lot further than a few plugs for your book. Most listeners tell me they bought a book based on how much fun I seemed to have interviewing a guest on my podcast rather than their elevator pitch. Trust me. It goes a long way. A lot longer than what the book is actually about.

Thank the podcaster afterward. Common courtesy is so nice in any environment. It doesn't have to be anything fancy. Taking a second to drop an email or a quick 'thanks for the great interview' on Skype before you disconnect works wonders for getting you back on the show. It might also help for future interviews, as podcasters talk to one another. A lot. I have a short list of the people over the years who were boring or talked over me or didn't do any of the common sense things outlined in this article.

Be a nice person and it comes back to you. Simple enough.

You're not done yet. Promote the episode when it goes live. Be proud you were on the podcast. Show your support of the podcast. Let your readers know it's live and you want them to listen to it. Hopefully new potential readers will see it, too.

Readers love active authors who promote. They like to know you haven't fallen off the edge of the world or are no longer writing. Out of sight and out of mind is a real thing in publishing. Be active and help spread the word.

Especially if you want to go back on the podcast in the future with your next release and garner even more readers for your career.

Podcasting is often overlooked or thought of as a very small part of the promoting game, but it is growing so quickly. It is another tool in your toolbox. Use it to your advantage and have fun doing it. Interacting with another person who's as passionate about reading and writing as you are is always fun no matter what.

Hopefully I'll be listening to your interviews soon, and maybe interviewing you myself.

Hiding in the Cracks Between Things

Kevin Lucia

originally published on sfsignal.com

My initial attempts at writing horror resulted in very obvious attempts to "scare" the reader. I had monsters—vampires, werewolves, demons—and I had blood and pumping viscera. There were incantations, tentacles, and "unspeakable horrors from beyond the grave." Frequently, I had awful people doing awful things, and awful things happening to those awful people as a consequence.

Though some of those early efforts glimmered with potential, most of them were cliché, on the nose, and very obvious "horror stories." Most of them were rejected, for which I'm very thankful, today. Luckily, I was new and clueless and convinced I was the second coming of Insert Horror Writer's Name Here, so I kept plugging away.

Eventually my technique improved. I learned how to end stories. I learned how to edit, learned word economy. I started selling stories here and there to small press, semi-pro venues. Some folks found them entertaining, and hey: progress was progress.

But about the time I turned down invitations to both a vampire and zombie anthology, thinking, "Geez, I don't WANT to write those kinds of stories," I began turning my thoughts toward the kind of stories I DID want to write. I'd accepted the horror genre as my own, if only because my stories didn't seem to fit anywhere else. Now I felt the need to stop writing stories for submissions calls, and start writing stories for me.

Around that time, horror legend Mort Castle—whom I'd studied under at Borderlands Press Writers' Bootcamp—offered me some advice during an email exchange. He'd praised me on reaching a certain point in my development as a writer in regards to technique and dialogue, but advised me that something was missing in my work, a personal voice unique to me. He then said words I'll never forget:

"The best stuff, the stuff that lasts, comes from our late night conversations with our very own selves."

Around then, I began reconnecting with an old favorite, Stephen King, and realized something I'd missed in my obsessive reading of his work in my twenties: what makes his stories so great and so universally loved by so many is their focus on the human element. We recognize his characters as people we KNOW. Maybe even recognize them as us...which can be more unsettling and horrifying than any mucus-laden, tentacled monster.

Along with this, I discovered Charles Grant, Ramsey Campbell, and T.M. Wright, and dug deep into the early, weird fiction of Ray Bradbury (*The October Country* especially), further shaping my focus. The very subtle ghost stories of M. R. James and Russell Kirk worked on my mind, also.

It was another year or two, however, before I really felt a key turn in my head. I was reading (not coincidentally) King's treatise on the horror genre, *Danse Macbre*. I came to his examination of *The Twilight Zone*, which I had begun viewing extensively. To be fair, King had his criticisms of TWZ, but this passage struck a huge chord within me:

"Week after week, The Twilight Zone presented ordinary people in extraordinary situations, people who had somehow turned sideways and slipped through a crack in reality...a powerful concept, and surely the clearest road into the land of fantasy for viewers and readers who do not ordinarily visit that land." – Stephen King, Danse Macbre

I thought to myself: Aha! Now THAT'S what I want to write!

I have since become a devotee to *The Twilight Zone*, and that "middle ground between light and shadow," featuring everyday folks we might meet on the street, has become my favorite place to tell stories. Another writer that King suggests in *Danse Macabre* achieves this even better than Serling is Jack Finney, in his collection of short stories, *The Third Level*. About Finney, King says:

"One of Finney's great abilities as a writer has been his talent for allowing his stories to slip unobtrusively, almost casually, across the line into another world..." – Stephen King, *Danse Macabre*

Like a good student, I hunted up a copy of *The Third Level* on Amazon.com...and was blown away. Though mostly time travel, dimension hopping tales and not horror, Finney's technique was as subtle and as smooth as King said. Here's what I wanted to write, stories I wanted to tell: human tales so universal that they'd speak to a wide range of people, drawing them in with their familiarity and simplicity...then twisting the world before they could escape.

Do my stories achieve this effect?

Even though I try, I'm sure they don't always. Does this mean I'll never write about monsters like vampires, werewolves, and zombies ever again? Certainly not. Each story is its own "boss," as Stephen King also likes to say.

However, I'm writing stories I care about, personally. Stories coming from inside me. About things hiding in the cracks, things which we're probably very fortunate never to see. And, most importantly, I'm having fun writing them, too, and when you write personally meaningful stories and are having fun doing it? That's something special, right there.

Writing Effective Scenes in Three Acts

Ben Eads

Google "How to write an effective scene" and you'll find pages of articles covering the elements listed below, but not much else. As opposed to only scratching the surface and naming the elements you need, let's examine a short horror story I made up for this article. We will keep these elements in mind, so we have a much deeper understanding of what makes an effective scene and how they come together to form the three acts of a story. Scenes should connect like Lego blocks, building the three acts of the story on a *strong* foundation. In this case, we'll use a simple, fast-paced short story as our example.

First, here are the elements:
- What is the purpose of the scene?
- What is the emotional focus?

- What back story do we gracefully insert into the moment that shows us instead of telling us important things about the character?
- What defining moments in your character's life follow them like a shadow?
- What is the internal conflict?
- What is the external conflict?
- What do we learn about your character?
- Do we genuinely care about your character?
- Most importantly, how does any of this information move the story forward?

These are what editors look for in your work. You would be amazed how many stories end up getting rejected because they lack these vital elements. Do you need all these elements when writing every single scene? No. Much of that depends on the location of the story and genre.

First, we need to know what the purpose of the opening scene is before we start writing. The opening scene should build the character up and give us the premise of the story itself. We'll also need back story gracefully inserted into the moment. Our opening scene begins with Cletus sitting beneath an ancient oak, as he loads rounds into his shotgun. Something hideous that lives in the forest has captured his wife and six-year-old daughter. He can hear his daughter screaming for him. He's preparing to rescue them, and, hopefully, kill what abducted them.

In this example, we have the purpose, backstory, emotional focus, empathy for the character, and the outer conflict. It's best to get this in the opening paragraphs. Some writers place them in the first paragraph, others within the first three. The opening paragraphs decides whether the editor stops reading your story or continues. Conflict is not a trivial thing, either. It should be high stakes. Reality is comprised by a series of moments we emotionally react to, challenge us, oppress us, or free us.

How does your character feel at the beginning of a scene and at the end of it? This will change your character. They'll either grow or fail, depending on the purpose of the scene/story.

Something must end in a scene, too. It could be a death, or the death of a plan your character had. Now they must re-group, face themselves, and try again. The latter builds suspense. Every event in your story should impact your main characters and encourage change. But it must be significant and serve the story. Now that we have our opening scene outlined, it's time to write the first act!

First act: We've already established purpose, built up your character, Cletus, his backstory as it pertains to plot, emotional focus, empathy for Cletus, and the outer conflict. Toward the end of the first act, Cletus will know a certain amount of information. Perhaps he wanders through the forest and finds an old, abandoned coal mine, with a dim light flickering within. He hears his daughter's scream again. This is where Cletus must face his inner fear, his inner struggle. Perhaps he is a push-over and cannot stand up for himself if his life depended on it. He must confront this internal conflict if he is to save his daughter. What makes him change? He knows this is his one and only chance to save his daughter, so he puts himself in the line of fire, even if it means he dies. The reason for this is yours to decide. See how we've raised the stakes here? Cletus has a plan. He'll go into the mine and fill the creature full of buckshot and save his daughter.

Second act: He enters the mine an gets lost. Everything has become more complicated, his emotions are at a fever pitch, and we are held captive, just like his daughter. Cletus must take a moment to think of a new strategy. His weaknesses are brought to the fore and he must conquer them. How will he? That's up to you. A gracefully inserted backstory into the moment will show us—as opposed to tell us—that his father used to own this mine, and Cletus tries to recall the stories his father told him about *why* the mine was shut down. Now he has some bearing and the home of this supernatural entity defined a little. He calls out to his daughter. She calls back. Now he knows where to go. But on the way, he finds the bodies of his best friends wrapped in what looks like spider-silk, rotting along the walls. This is where the defining moments in Cletus's life come in to play. The moments that made him who he is. He will come in conflict with this. How and when is up you. Then he sees his wife strung up, just like the rest of them, but she's alive. She imparts a vital piece of information to him: Where the supernatural entity is and where their daughter is. She also gives us a little insight into *why* the creature does this. Best to give just a little insight, or none at all. It's up to you to decide the *why* and *what*. However, he must make a choice between saving his wife or his daughter. In a very emotional moment, his wife tells him he has to save their daughter. That's what matters. This tears his heart in two. He knows it's the right thing to do, but there is a price to pay for it. How does this change your character? How does this emotionally connect the inner struggle to outer struggle? Again, that's your choice.

Third act: Cletus has made his choice. He will save their daughter, clutching the thought he can save both of them, and their lives can go back to normal. This idea, while noble, is because of his fear of losing what he loves most. How does this change Cletus? This is where Cletus's flaws get in the way of his goal. How does he continue? What defining moment in his life has given him the potential to rise above all odds? Then, and only then, will we have our climax: Cletus locates and frees his daughter from the spider webs and carries her away from this place, so he can save his wife, too. Enter the antagonist: a supernatural entity. The antagonist reminds Cletus his daughter may or may not survive chemotherapy, despite her beating the cancer thus far. He has a much better ever-after for her. Introducing his daughter's fight with cancer into the third act keeps the emotional elements of the story growing and alive and thickens the plot. Richard Matheson is one of the kings of doing this. You could have inserted this information at the end of the second act, when he meets his wife. Again, that's up to you. The antagonist offers Cletus the opportunity to join his wife and daughter in this amazing ever-after, where cancer will never kill his daughter. That way they can be a family again. The antagonist is justified, not just some cookie-cutter villain. The choice Cletus makes is up to you. After all, this is horror, and it could go a few different ways. Regardless of where you take the story, the ending must resolve the inner struggle and the outer struggle. Both are emotionally tied together. Then we will have a satisfying climax and ending.

Obviously, every story is different, as the example I've given you shows. But what all stories have in common are three acts, and each act is comprised of scenes. As you start to draft the story, keeping asking yourself: Why? Being a good detective makes good fiction. Even the best of outlines give way to the story writing itself. After getting that story idea, you can start inquiring and thinking about these elements *before* you begin to write.

However, I wouldn't burden yourself too much. The rough draft is where you just get it out. Drafting is where you should see these elements weaving together and forming a story a reader can't put down. You can start slowly, if you wish, by drafting the story with only one of these elements in mind. That way it won't feel like you're moving a boulder, more like moving small rocks. The more fiction you write, the more time you'll save by nailing these fundamental elements within the rough draft. It's like lifting weights. Start with the light ones, building up muscle as you go along, so you can lift the heavy weights.

Please have patience. They say it's a virtue for a reason. If it takes you a year to write a novella, then so be it. Remind yourself that the story is in charge, not you. Never you. Try bending a story to your whim and watch it blow up in your face. Write with these elements in mind and watch the story flourish. Once you're finished drafting the story down to incorporate these elements, hit up a good beta reader to critique it. Or, even better, hire a professional editor who has worked in the horror genre for some time to edit it. Then draft it down again, fixing everything they caught. Again, patience. Once you've satisfied this editor, it's time to submit the story to the best presses out there.

Rejection Grace

Kelli Owen

As a writer, you should keep this word in the back of your head at all times: Grace. Publishers, editors, and yes, readers, will easily spot those who either don't understand the definition or the *need* to hold this word dear.

What am I talking about? I'm talking about how writers react to—and *gasp* *respond* to—rejections. Because whether you've published one story or one hundred stories, there's *never* a reason to not be professional. Never a reason to not show or have grace.

You see, there are those who write and there are those who publish. That first group is quite content to scribble volumes for their own eyes and never ever put it out there for the public. And then there are those of us who are mildly sadistic at best and may actually enjoy torture at worst. We submit our words for publication and then pace, while waiting to hear back from an opinion we purposely asked for.

Are we always happy with that opinion? No. Should we have a tantrum, whine, bitch, piss or moan? Hell no. The golden rule of rejections? You absolutely should not, under any circumstances, ever *ever* do either of these two things: respond to the rejection or whine about it publicly.

That first faux pas? Responding? No. Just no. It's that simple. Don't. Why would you? You do *nothing* to change the mind of the editor who sent you the rejection (and keep in mind, on some level you should be thankful for receiving notice in the first place, since many publications only contact you if you're accepted).

"Oh but I just want to say thank you." No. The editor had to read a lot more than just *your* story. If you respond, even to say thank you, you are wasting their valuable time. *"But they were wrong about something in the story, a.k.a. misunderstood my intent, a.k.a. blah blah I need to stick up for my story because blah."* No. And if you think they won't remember that, you're wrong. If you think they won't tell their editing and publishing friends, you're wrong. Slowly, for those in the back, do not—do (period) not (period)—respond to a rejection. Ever.

And that second one? *Seriously*? Let me just remind all of you of one tiny, very *very* important fact of life as we now know it: the Internet is *forever*. Don't believe me? Go ahead and look. May I suggest waybackmachine.com? But also, and more immediately, screenshots have become the law of the land.

Recently, I watched as an anthology sent out their rejections and triggered group hysteria in the form of an en masse Internet response showcasing all the authors who were either never told, or whom outright *chose* to ignore the golden rules. Suddenly there were (more than a few) people posting online, openly, angrily, about how they were going to *make their own* anthology out of all their rejected submissions from this one.

Re-read that. Slower.

Yes, you read that right. And the editor responded beautifully—telling them to feel free to do so, as it will be the worst thing no one's ever read. I laughed. Oh my god, did I laugh. I mean, I gasped at the brazen willingness to knowingly damage their own careers. But then I laughed, because *wow*.

Once more, for those in the back: the Internet is forever.

And while your antics may not make it to the screenshot hall of shame, those you annoy with less-than-professional behavior *will* tell others, sharing your foibles with all their editing and publishing friends. As I write this, there are currently three different threads on my various social medias discussing someone who reacted poorly in public. Three. Today. And that's just in *my* little corner.

While the publishing world is a massive entity, the area we call our genre is a small island of misfits. It's not quite a family, though parts can feel like it. The rest is neighbors and friends and coworkers. And while the circles can seem tight-knit and closed off to the outside eye, most are quite welcoming, if not fluid to those around it. At the end of the day, the lesson is: it's far too small a community to think you can do anything remotely close to responding or reacting, and not have it become a scary lesson whispered to newbies—to frighten them as they're tucked in at night.

Grace, people.

Find it. Hold it tight. Never let it go.

Remember, a rejection isn't a statement on you as a person—it just means *that* story, at *that* point in time, for *that* publication didn't work. It doesn't even necessarily mean the story sucked. And it certainly doesn't mean you should respond or react.

If you are rejected, look at why. If they sent a form letter, it may simply be that it didn't fit the theme or feel or gore factor or whatever other thread connects the accepted stories. If they were kind enough to tell you why and there's a critique or suggestion, look at it with open eyes, consider it heavily, and then adjust and/or edit as you need or agree. Either way, with or without comments, your job at this point is not to say thank you, it's not to whine on your social media, it's to resubmit the story. Get it out the door. No rejected story should ever spend the night. They are not welcome company, but rather relatives who don't know when to leave.

Except when they need to be grounded, such as when it was written for a very specifically themed anthology. I have seen what happens to the market after a themed anthology sends out their rejections—because once upon a time, many of us giggled and gasped in horror, as every open submission call received rejected stories about "pirate cats from outer space." No, rejections from specific themes need to sit for a bit—maybe forever. Some can be reshaped into something more generic, some cannot, but that's a whole different lesson.

Dallas (Jack Ketchum) once told me the most important words ever when it comes to a rejection, "Move on. They have." Wise, wise words, from a wise, wise man.

For those who need it, maybe put a post-it note on your screen, keyboard, wall, whatever—wherever you'll see it. You can write his words verbatim. Or you can write "Don't respond, don't react." Or you could even write "Be professional." Or you can reduce it all down to just that one really important word. Say it with me… Grace.

A Writer Prepares

John Palisano

B e the tree. Be the wind. Be the universe. We've all heard the riffs and jokes about acting classes by now, haven't we? The fun part? It's based on some truth.

During Film School at Emerson College in Boston, I was speaking with Professor Pete Chvany outside the film department. The question was breached: "How do I learn to work with actors?"

"Go be an actor," Pete said, with his usual candor and effectiveness.

I did. And it was one of the best things I'd done as a storyteller up until that time in my life.

Going into those classes, I was a nervous wreck. Absolutely terrified. Sweating like a hog in the slaughter line. Before we did anything else, our teacher had us close our eyes and imagine we were someone we were close to. It could be anybody, but we had to try and embody their skin, inside out. This was my introduction to Method Acting. It has helped me find characters in all of my published work. I use many of the same tools I learned in acting class to develop characters in my stories.

FIFTY QUESTIONS

One of the toughest assignments in developing a character for an actor are the fifty questions. What is this? It's simply a list of fifty questions you explore when developing your character. They start out easy, but get more challenging. Where were you born? What year? Who are your parents? Your family? Your favorite food? Favorite color? Easy, right? But they soon progress to things like who the first person was that broke your heart. The questions make you think. Make you really know the person. The goal is to know them as well as you know yourself. There are many different versions of the Acting Character Development Questions out there.

So, what do you do once you have completed your fifty questions? You have options. What if you have more than one leading character? Do you do a fifty questions for each leading character in your story? That's up to you, but I have done so for most of my books and short stories. There are so many books and classes centering on world building. Most are focused on the intricacies of a fantasy world. What do people eat? What are the politics? What do people do as far as money and exchanges? What are the details of their religions? How do they build homes? How do they get around? One of the biggest complaints about epic stories we see are that the characters are flat, or that audiences have a hard time relating to them. Maybe that's due to the fact that the world building stopped with the castles and spaceships and alien societies. But by using the tools actors have developed, you can build their psychological world, and make it dimensional and real and relatable.

149

Warning! Even though you may go through all of those questions, and develop rich backstories, you may be tempted to want to put all that hard-thought-out research into your story. Resist that temptation. The backstories and psychology inform the characters in ways that make them real and pop off the page. When we first meet people, we don't learn every single thing about them right away. Things are revealed over time. Some things never need to be in the actual story, but can help you in ways you may not realize.

HURDLES

One of the biggest hurdles storytellers face is writer's block. In my own experience, almost every time I've hit a wall, it's because I don't understand what a character would do in that situation, or the scene somehow rings false and shuts me down. One of the biggest tools I use as a storyteller when I hit those walls is to take a step back and think through the scene as the character. In effect, using method acting to inhabit the character to see through the moment. If it's not clear, I know I need to do some more homework on that character.

BAD ACTORS

What about bad actors? This is a great time to chat about how this can all go terribly wrong. We've all seen stiff actors. Actors who seem to suck the life out of a scene by their very presence. Often, these aren't trained individuals, or they simply aren't wired to inhabit a character. Believe it or not, many bad actors are extremely intelligent people. What I've seen happen is they are trying to process every line with all the backstory and weight they think belongs there, slowing them down, and making them appear wooden. Remember how we discussed not everything you think of needs to be present in every scene? This is a perfect example. It's good to forget about as much of what you develop and just let it all hang in the background. That's the magic trick good actors pull off. They have learned, through lots of experience, how to find that crucial balance. It's much harder than it appears. A naturalistic performance is one of the most sought after, yet most challenging goals of any actor or storyteller. Here are a few tips on how to get there.

CHOICES

Actors think a lot about choices. Remember those fifty questions? When you were going through them, were you making interesting, uncommon choices? The first time you go through them, it's often easier to lean on simple, time worn answers. For example: Batman's backstory has been repeated countless times. It's very well known. When a villain appears and does something to trigger Batman—adding a detail previously unknown about his parents, let's say—we are all emotionally there with him. It's interesting because of that. We are engaged. We feel the mixed emotions. We are THAT familiar with his story. Even though we know logically what should happen, we understand and feel the underlying emotion of the character.

On the flip side, if we make boring, well worn choices for the backstories for our developing characters, they'll come off uninteresting, dull and lifeless. An interesting choice may be key to really bringing a character to life. Here's an example I used: I had to play a long dialogue scene. There didn't seem to be much going on. But, when the scene was analyzed, the couple were meeting after a long time apart, and a bad breakup. It was the first time they'd seen one another. They were just exchanging pleasantries before heading in to see a mutual friend. The words themselves were not interesting. The script didn't have much in the way of context. I chose to have my character nervously touching his ring finger while they spoke; her presence brought to the fore the absence of their wedding ring on his finger, and instinctively, he sought some sort of physical comfort during the exchange. It was subtle. But it gave the weight to the words necessary to make the scene more emotionally true.

I once interviewed a well-known actor. We spoke way beyond our allotted time and questions. I joked about how his character always had corny one-liners in the franchise, and how that must have been hard to deal with. How naive I was! He told me that he was taken aback when he first received the scripts. He thought about how he'd have to infuse them with some sort of weight, other than just performing schtick. He came up with a horrifying backstory for the jokes. Each one was a joke the character's father would tell him right before beating him as a kid. That way, the jokes came out sinister in a way that went below the surface, and allowed the actor to dig in hardcore. It worked. Big time. For me? That was a huge learning moment, and it's something I think about often in my own creative journey. One can always find a way to turn something that seems mediocre at first glance and spin it into something true and real. That's one of the reasons we have often heard a great actor can 'elevate' an otherwise average movie. It's all inside those details.

WHAT'S MY MOTIVATION?
Which brings us to motivation. Why does a character want something? And what is it that they want? If this isn't strong, then the story will suffer. Defeating the bad guy is a given. We can strengthen that motivation with character building. If we know where a person came from, we can zero in on where they'd like to go. There are so many wonderful possibilities to explore. There are at least two

different wants a character will have at any given time. The first is what they want immediately in the scene. Maybe they just want a drink and there is a line at the McDonald's, and they only have a few minutes or they'll be late. That may not be a big deal for the immediate scene. But what will they be late for? What if they've been late dozens of times and their job is hanging in the balance? That changes the stakes of the scene. They want a drink...need that drink...but they can't be late. That will completely change the performance, or how you write the scene. If they're unemployed, there's really no long term motivation for them, or us, by proxy, to be worried about. If we amp it up, and we see that our person always seems to be late because of things outside their control, it makes us like them more. Or we think it's funny. If he is always stopping to rescue a cat, or give someone a jump start, or something along those lines, it's hilarious. And we can explore why this person is this way. Maybe they left seminary school, but they are still unable to walk away from a person in need. Maybe someone walked away from them or a loved one during a moment of need that had disastrous consequences. When we blend all these factors, the character comes alive and we understand them. They are more than just a pawn moving our story goals and actions forward. They become dimensional. They become real. We, as storytellers, understand them. With that in mind, if we are inside that McDonald's, waiting in that line, and knowing what we know now, let's introduce a wrinkle. Someone busts in, guns out, and grabs Mrs. Thompson around the neck from behind and points that gun at her head, shouting he's going to take her out if everyone doesn't hand over their cash. Well, we know the kind of person we have in our main character. You can pretty much predict how they're going to react and act. That's because you've built enough of a backstory to know them as well as you know any character you've ever loved.

The good part to this? Knowing the characters at this level is one of the best ways to combat writer's block.

That's just one small example and exercise, but I bet you get the idea.

In summary, there are some wonderfully rich tools from the acting world storytellers in many different formats can use. These are tried and true techniques that can really open up new worlds, and also help you to find the many layers of your characters, and to enrich your storytelling toolbox in a really fun and satisfying way.

Break a leg!

An Interview with Mort Castle

Joe Mynhardt

Joe Mynhardt: What would you consider the biggest pitfall for young authors today?

Mort Castle: When I was comin' up, it was hard to get published.

It still is.

However, now thanks to, ahem, self-publication, indie authorness, ebooks, Kindle, Nook, Swindle, and Shmuck, why, we've eliminated those nasty gate-keeping editors and publishers and everyone can be published... That is, everyone can delude himself that he has been published because he threw some words onto a computer screen and transferred them to some ebook platform, where those words, many of them fairly close to English, will be read only by indulgent mothers who never learned about tough love and aspiring self-publishing writers (right) who will imitate this "get it while it's free and worth every penny" success.

Oh, thou doth protest, I have all my beta readers...

Who far too often know even less than the guy who seeks their opinion:

"You story is really good."

"Why do you say that?"

"Because I like it."

"Why do you like it?"

"Because it's good."

The hamster runs all night in its exercise wheel and still gets nowhere.

Truly never has it been so easy for so many to be so self-deluded and to aid others in becoming no less deluded.

My advice to my students—and all genuinely aspiring writers: Learn to write. Writing is a craft and a craft can be learned and a craft can be taught.

Worry less about "platforms" and "social media" and "emerging technology" and thus and such.

You've got to have a product before you can sell it. Don't delay learning how to make that product by throwing slapdash alleged thoughts into your endless "Tall Zombie" series of novels destined to be read by Aunt Phoebe and perhaps a tall zombie or two.

Joe: How did your fascination with the horror genre start, and what about it continues to draw you in?

Mort: Thank you, Mrs. Curlin, my third grade teacher at Delano School on Chicago's West Side. She brought in the latest high tech educational media, a long playing phonograph record, and we eight year olds sat and listened to "The Telltale Heart" and "The Pit and the Pendulum," and we were horrified.

Play that today and you'd have 23 school psychologists and a platoon of lawyers on the scene. *These traumatized kids will be wetting the bed for decades*

I was enthralled and not traumatized because somehow horror pushed the right buttons in my psyche and soul.

It scares so good!

My friend, F. Paul Wilson, a writer of thrillers, mysteries, science-fiction, and horror, has said he thinks the affinity for horror is hard-wired. It's DNA. I tend to agree with that.

All kids have nightmares (just like adults). I was one of those kids who had 'em and liked 'em.

So, when I started writing in a fooling around way and then seriously, why jumping into the horror pool was just as natural as a frog plopping into the pond. It was where I belonged—and still belong. Usually, anyway.

Joe: Tell us more about your own writing method. Any rituals or location/mood preferences before you get started?

Mort: Great question. I used to have all sorts of rituals, including having two or three typewriters (yeah, I am old!) set up in different areas so that if my work on the short story "The Telltale Tale Told by a Toad" suddenly hit that brick wall, I could move on to the typewriter that had my poetry cycle, "Perverse Verse for Petty Perverts," and if that one went South with its similes, I could go to my latest novel, *For Whom the Bell Gongs*.

Hats, used to have all sorts of writing hats.

And, yes, I used to smoke. I smoked like a champ. Two to three packs a day. I used to smoke in the shower; I liked the challenge. So next to the typewriter (and later Kaypro II computer) I had an ashtray the size of a skating rink. I'd smoke about three or four cigarettes and stare at the blank paper (later screen) until I felt all kinds of synapses connected by nicotine spider webs, and then... Launch time! Stop when the ashtray is overflowing.

But now, with age, my rituals have changed.

I avoid writing whenever possible. The more I learned about craft, the higher I set the bar in my attempt to create ART! I hope I am not being pretentious, but if it's just *a forget it two seconds after you read it* story, why the hell do I want to waste time out of my life writing it?

And I can avoid writing real well. I can spend time with a wonderful wife as we watch the birds hit the banquet in our backyard feeders. I can play guitar or banjo or any of my forty or fifty instruments. I really love television nowadays. Love theater and movies.

I don't write until I am seized by something that makes me say, "This concept could possess me and become my obsession and I will tackle the goddamned thing. And for a bit, I'm feeling young again..."

And then the ritual. Hemingway spoke of knowing he could make the story happen when he had his one true sentence. I am harder to convince. I need my one true paragraph. And if I get that, sometimes after sweating blood, bullets, and bullshit for days, I will commit to writing the whole thing.

Not fun, though. Not. But as some other writer put it (yeah, I steal: makes me a good researcher), "I hate writing, but I love having written."

Joe: What character traits do you believe you have that make you a unique author? And how would you recommend young authors present their own personality and character traits in their work?

Mort: I am not the devil, but I know I contain multitudes. I write true to what I know to be true to the human condition, the human condition that has been my lot since I got my diploma in humanness: my birth certificate. I follow Langston Hughes's dictum: Let the poem come out of you /

then it will be true.

Young writers, hey guys, even though I love TV and film and even books, your best bet is spending long hours in serious conversation with the guy who lives in your mirror.

Yeah, that's the advice: "Turn off the media. Get real!"

Get real.

Remember that old one, WRITE ABOUT WHAT YOU KNOW.

And you can trust your own thoughts, feelings, experiences, and fantasies to give you more authenticity than you will get through the media's high tech filters.

Joe: What advice do you have for young authors? Perhaps something you wish you'd done or learned early on in your career.

Mort: I was publishing in the mid-60s. I realized that I could aim at making that capitalized ART in the mid-1980s, when several people I respected as artists said something like, "There are flashes of something more than pop-pulp-pap in your writing. You might want to consider taking yourself seriously and really reaching." They had to tell me that often. Repeatedly. And then, I began to say, *Maybe*. And eventually I could think of myself as an artist—and hope that the world might come to see me as one.

So, that's my advice. Push aside the delusions. Ignore the Twitter twaddle and Facebook follies. If you're 13, 23, or 67, do it for real, if you have that sort of desire. Do it for real. You are not puffing yourself up if you say, "Yeah, I want my story to be around 300 years after I am not." It's not how many books you've slapped onto Kindle that will bring you—let's say it—IMMORTALITY.

Hey, just like Ray Bradbury, you can Live Forever!

The Seven Steps to Mastery
For Horror Writers

Bret McCormick

" **A** piece about writing schlock / the 80s would be terrific—new authors will have much to learn from you!" This was the mandate given me by James Longmore at Hellbound Books, when he asked me to be part of this nonfiction project for aspiring horror writers. His only other caveat was that the piece should be under 5,000 words. With these instructions in mind, I'll embrace this opportunity to hold forth.

In some circles, I will be forever associated with "schlock" and the 1980s because I created a plethora of no-budget feature films during the heyday of home video. My movies were peddled all over the planet, banned in some countries, placed on the 'video nasties' list in others and freely exploited in places like the US and Japan. In 1986 I made a movie called *The Abomination*. This grim, ragged piece of cinema still maintains a devoted cult following around the world. Just last year I was interviewed by Rurik Salle regarding *The Abomination* for a French language print publication called Distorsion Dictature (Distortion Dictatorship).

Some people consider *The Abomination* art. Others maintain it's schlock. I don't feel the need to distinguish between the two. Could be both are right. Though it doesn't contain any punk rock music, I think of *The Abomination* as 'punk cinema,' born from the same dissatisfaction and angst that fueled the work of the Ramones and Patti Smith.

From 1984 to 1996 I was involved with some twenty one exploitation movies—all but one shot in Texas. At a party celebrating my 59th birthday, author E.R. Bills overheard me discussing my schlock cinema days with fellow schlockmeister, Glen Coburn. "This needs to be a book!" Bills exclaimed. With some persistent prodding on his part I managed to put together my first nonfiction book—*Texas Schlock: B-Movie Sci Fi and Horror from the Lone Star State*. It's a popular item with film geeks (and every family has at least one of those).

To date, I've published three novels: *Hellfire, Headhunters from Outer Space* and *Skin Dreams (Poor White Trash Part 3)*. I've published somewhere in the neighborhood of fifteen short stories, mostly horror, but Saturday Evening Post published two of my humorous pieces. I have edited three anthologies of horror fiction and co-edited, with E.R. Bills, another couple. I've completed one nonfiction book, which I mentioned above. This is not an enormous body of work for a man in his sixties, but I really got serious about writing in March 2014. All of this work was done after that date, so within the past five years.

In a nutshell, these are my bonafides. These are the reasons Mr. Longmore thought someone might want to read what I have to say on the subject of writing. I am flattered to be asked to contribute to this volume. May you find something here that serves you well in your own literary endeavors.

Now, that I've introduced myself, let's talk about writing.

Nothing happens in a vacuum. All things are related, woven together like threads in a skein of cloth. In fact, every thing you think of as a 'thing' is not a thing at all, but a process. So let me describe a bit of the process that brought me to where I am.

I have always loved words. Rhymes, synonyms, etymologies and puns have fascinated me for as long as I can remember. My mother and both my grandmothers read to me when I was too young to read to myself. I'm sure this helped. At the age of ten I learned that people actually got paid to write stories (the lucky ones, anyway). From that time forward I focused on developing my writing skills. Throughout my public education, I was lauded for my literary ability. When I was thirteen, a family friend read one of my stories and said, "Bret, if you want to be a writer, I think you should drop out of high school and write full time." My mother was flabbergasted. I hung in there, but by the time I graduated, I realized the public school system had taught me precious little that would propel me forward in my aspirations.

Though writing was my first love, I was seduced away from her by a harlot called filmmaking. Early on I formed the half-baked notion that I wanted to make movies for my cinematic icon, Roger Corman. I made two films for Roger: *Rumble in the Streets* and *The Protector*. Immediately after attaining my goal, I abandoned the film industry. People have asked me why I stopped making movies.

Until 1996, I'd led something of a charmed existence. Life was a game I played without taking it too seriously. I was a naïve aesthete, dancing through my days with reckless abandon. That all changed. I experienced a two-

and-a-half-year period of increasingly traumatic personal tragedies. I responded by dropping out. Of everything. I read a lot, meditated a lot, slept and worked just enough to survive.

I mention this chapter of my life because it dynamically shaped my approach to writing. The fundamental reexamination of all my values shifted my perspective into previously uncharted territory. Like a lot of folks who've experienced overwhelming grief, I began searching for a deeper meaning to my life. I was looking for that little guy behind the curtain, pulling levers and growling into the microphone, the one responsible for the big spectacle I'd experienced. All my attention was turned toward metaphysical pursuits, esoteric knowledge, spiritual pathways of enlightenment. My reaction was not unusual. Many people will respond to tragedy in much the same way. In fact, it's become something of a cliché. Most will be lured back to the 'real world' by the demands of work, family pressure or the simple need to reembrace the familiar. Not me. When I turned that corner, I went all the way and never looked back.

My explorations led me to discover a world I'd been trained to believe was only fantasy. The paranormal experiences I encountered both expanded my consciousness and emboldened me. It's about here that I can imagine some readers rolling their eyes and perhaps skipping ahead to the next chapter, Please, follow your heart. Everything I'm discussing here has a direct bearing on my approach to writing. In my experience, many horror writers are more open to the paranormal than the general public, so it's my hope some of you will bear with me.

Continue reading beyond this point and you have successfully negotiated the first gauntlet.

"There is some confusion as to what magic actually is. I think this can be cleared up if you just look at the very earliest descriptions of magic. Magic in its earliest form is often referred to as "the art". I believe this is completely literal. I believe that magic is art and that art, whether it be writing, music, sculpture, or any other form is literally magic. Art is, like magic, the science of manipulating symbols, words, or images, to achieve changes in consciousness."

- Alan Moore

If you don't know who Alan Moore is, google him. I agree with Mr. Moore's assessment, not in some figurative, metaphorical way, but quite literally. Every time we create a story that others can lose themselves in, we are performing a magical act.

In March 2014 I hit a turning point in my life. I gave up drinking alcohol because I felt it was leading me down a path of complacence and confusion. Simultaneously, I began writing daily. After decades of fantasizing about writing a novel, including a couple of failed starts with NaNoWriMo, I committed to actually completing a work of at least 80,000 words. The only obstacles were the ones in my head. I had a strange epiphany. It occurred to me that I needed to give myself permission to write a bad novel. My goal was not to write a bad novel, but if I gave myself permission to be less than brilliant the first time out, I'd be empowered to complete the process. Above my computer, I tacked a sign to the wall. It read, "Everyone has the right to write. Your novel does not have to be great (or even good) to be published. Just write."

Seeing that sign every day encouraged me. Let my first bit of advice be, **Give Yourself Permission to Fail.** You'll learn from your mistakes. Mistakes actually accelerate growth. Keep moving forward. Don't let seeming failures keep you from writing. Many of the most astounding works of literature look like grotesque mistakes when examined through the lens of established literary rules.

I jumped into the novel-writing process with both feet. The result was a piece called *Hellfire*. I let the story pour out of my unconscious, with no planning, no outlines, no conscious attempts to create layers of meaning. I just wrote. When it was completed, I was gratified to find, on closer examination of my work, there were in fact esoteric threads woven into the names and events of the story. Things I would not have consciously decided to include. I had learned that my unconscious is a much better writer than my conscious mind. I just needed to trust that vast occult part of my consciousness.

This leads us to my second rule of writing. On second thought, it's not a rule so much as a suggestion, a clue, an invitation to explore a great mystery: **Write from your Gut.** Don't be a slave to form or the expectations of others. There's plenty of fascinating stuff lurking in the shadows of your mind, you just have to find the door and let it out.

When you sit at the keyboard and just let the story flow out of you, without the continual kibitzing of your everyday ego, you allow yourself to create a grander and more unified work. Why? Because your unconscious mind is infinitely greater than your conscious mind. Just let the story pour out. There will be plenty of time for nitpicking and second-guessing later. The world is full of folks who'll be more than happy to bring your story into alignment with the mainstream narrative. If you're as sharp as I hope you are, you'll disregard them. Especially in the realm of horror, you need to operate outside the mainstream box.

Speaking of 'horror,' let's indulge in an aside and explore that, shall we?

What is horror?

Wikipedia says this about horror fiction: "**Horror** is a genre of speculative fiction which is intended to frighten, scare, disgust, or startle its readers by inducing feelings of horror and terror. Literary historian J. A. Cuddon defined the horror story as "a piece of fiction in prose of variable length...which shocks, or even frightens the reader, or perhaps induces a feeling of repulsion or loathing." It creates an eerie and frightening atmosphere. Horror is frequently supernatural, though it might be also non-supernatural. Often the central menace of a work of horror fiction can be interpreted as a metaphor for the larger fears of a society."

Basically, this tells us horror fiction is intended to disturb the reader. Why? Why do we want to disturb our readers and why would these readers wish to be disturbed? These are big questions.

First, I'd say what frightens me may not frighten you. There are an incredible number of personality types on the planet with a correspondingly large list of fear responses. Consequently, one person's horror is another person's melodrama. Some folks are living in such neatly structured, well-insulated circumstances it takes very little in the way of imaginative fiction to frighten or disturb them. Others are so jaded, it's rare for them to feel the least discomfort when reading even the most extreme horror tales. Both have something in common: in order for horror to have its effect on them, they must be afraid of something. They must feel they have something to lose.

Life is the most obvious thing we may be anxious about losing. If we've been subjected to a particular type of religious training, we may be even more frightened of losing something we call the soul. H.P. Lovecraft, one of the stand-out American writers of horror, believed humankind's greatest fear was "fear of the unknown." Humans are an insecure bunch and they've devised an

amazing number of strategies to convince themselves they have all the answers. This provides an emotional comfort zone, allowing them to function in daily life without the burden of fearing that which they do not know. The truth is there is much more to the universe than we can grasp at present.

*"To paraphrase J. B. S. Haldane: Our situation may not only be stranger than we suppose; it may be stranger than we **can** suppose."*
- **Terence McKenna**

Being a human in this vast universe of unknown things can easily make us feel like castaways drifting in the vast Pacific Ocean, on a tiny inflatable raft with little food and no tools to help us find our way home. This is the fear we hide from ourselves every day. This is why many of us are willing to trade the terrifying solitude and its unanswered questions for jobs we hate, superficial, unsatisfying relationships and any other distraction that will carry our minds away from the overwhelming uncertainty that is our true birthright. This is why we drink and drug ourselves into oblivion.

What is horror to you? Examine your deepest fears and write about them in the rawest manner possible. Don't whistle in the dark. Don't bluff the reader with false bravado. Let the detective fiction folks cover that front. Horror needs to be a place of gut-wrenching, desperate honesty if it is to remain horror, if it is to strike nerves with a truth your readers will acknowledge.

Continuing on, I've placed **Write from your Gut** in position number two on my list, but this third suggestion is equally important. **Write on a Regular Schedule.**

A major battle for writers is won simply by showing up. Your presence on the battlefield causes those ghostly naysayers flitting about in your head to flee. Everyone has heard of muses. They were popularized by Greek mythology. They exist. For real. Not as a cool metaphor for some mundane mental process that leads to inspiration. The space around you is teeming with disembodied entities who would love to help you with your writing. If you set your intent and seat yourself at the keyboard at the same time every day, it's much easier for them to reach across the great divide and find you. Being punctual is important, not because our spectral friends operate on a schedule—quite the contrary. The world they inhabit is timeless. However, keeping a routine is an expression of intent. *Intent rules the universe.* If your intention is strong enough to hold you to a schedule, it will shine like a beacon, attracting helpful influences from beyond.

The Greeks believed no man was a genius, but he could have a relationship with one. I agree with their assessment.

Are you thinking to yourself, *"This McCormick guy's more than a bit woo woo! He's gone 'round the bend! Where's that white jacket?"*

Continue reading, and you will have met and overcome the second gauntlet.

Item number four on my list concerns what most of us refer to as an ego. Regarding the ego: Have one. Own it. So, let's call this instruction, **Honor Your Ego.** Admit that you have an individuated and powerful will, then exercise it.

Today, political correctness has been extended to such a ludicrous extreme, I find it difficult to take seriously. Especially for an artist of any kind. The underlying message seems to be, you are an inconsequential invertebrate, stay in your shell. All this talk of trigger words and rhetoric designed to pit sexes and sexual persuasions against one another seems foolish to me. If you want to be an inoffensive, neutral mollusk, go right ahead.

See where it gets you. Good writing will always contain something offensive to someone, somewhere. And, by God, you've got a right to your potentially offensive narrative.

As I write these words, the president of the United States is Donald Trump. He's not my idea of what a good president should be. He is superior to all of his recent predecessors in one regard: he doesn't give two shits about political correctness. This is a divine intervention in my opinion. Trump is here to remind us that we've gone off the rails with that PC crap. For me, the point is well-taken. For the record, I am not a Trump supporter. I did not vote for him. I am watching his legacy unfold with keen interest, however. In your writing, be as brash as Trump when expressing your ideas. The summits of literary mastery are not attained by the timid.

Attack the reader. Do not aim for lulling them into a sense of security. They might fall asleep. If you're writing horror, you want to leave them incapable of sleep.

It takes a certain amount of ego to believe you have something to say that others should take the time to read. Be strong enough to tell your story from your perspective. If you try to conform to some generic, homogenized narrative foisted upon you by pop psychology and the culture police you'll create a forgettable hodge podge of no lasting value. Trust your instincts. Don't be dissuaded from the vision at your core, no matter how tarnished, jagged and unpopular that vision may be.

The differences in your writing, not the conformities, will make your work memorable.

"If the audience knew what they needed, then they wouldn't be the audience. They would be the artists. It is the job of artists to give the audience what they need."
- **Alan Moore**

Ignore both critics and those who praise your work. This is instruction number five. By ignore, I don't mean completely disregard the opinions of others. Thank them for their assessment of your work, good or bad, then go on your way. Don't take praise or condemnation to heart. If you do, these will influence your future choices as a writer. You want your influences coming from your core, not from out there somewhere.

In 1981, I took a continuing education course on Creative Writing at the local community college. The class was taught by Warren Norwood. Norwood was a wooly gnome of a man whose science fiction novel, **The Windhover Tapes**, had been published by Bantam Books. Norwood's presentation was fun and memorable.

One night he talked about criticism and not letting it impact your determination. "Folks," he said, "opinions are like assholes. Everybody's got one and they all stink."

At this point, a polite little lady in the back row, chimed in, "And polite people don't discuss theirs in public."

I still laugh to myself when this memory resurfaces.

Everyone has an opinion. Everyone is entitled to his/her opinion. But they are all equal on their face. No one opinion should be held above any other, with one exception: *yours*. If you write a story or novel that *you* would enjoy reading, had you discovered it in some discarded paperback or on a website somewhere, then you have done your job. If you honestly like, or better yet love, your story, then you have done your job as an author. No writer could do more.

Number six on my list is **Publish.**

If you're writing short stories, constantly send them out to appropriate venues. In the history of the human race, there has never been a time when it was easier to get your work published. Admittedly, most markets do not pay much. If you so decide, you can submit only to the top

paying markets. Be prepared for a lot of waiting and rejection, if you take this path.

To my way of thinking, it's better to be publishing things all along, rather than waiting for that big score. The more stuff you have out there, the more seriously you will be taken as a writer. More importantly, all writing exists to be read. You want people reading your work. That is priority one.

If you've written a novel and you're tired of waiting for 'reputable' publishers to recognize its worth, then you should self-publish. Amazon and friends have made this very easy for you. If you create your own cover design and publish exclusively in electronic format, it won't cost you a penny to put your work out there. Personally, I like having paperback editions of my work to sell people. You'll find many book stores and organizations of various descriptions are willing, eager even, to have a local author present their work and do a reading and/or book signing. Start small if you have to, but start. If you truly are a writer, you'll build momentum along the way.

How do you know if you're truly a writer? If it makes you feel good. There are few things in life that give me more pleasure than writing. It's my favorite part of the day.

Write, write, write and publish, publish, publish.

Given the opportunity, people (at least some of them) will read your work. In order to read your stuff, people have to know it exists. That won't happen if your manuscript remains a file on the hard drive of your computer. Even if your work is published, it will become part of the vast tidal wave of data potential readers must sift through in order to discover your brilliance. Like a salmon swimming upstream to spawn, your story will have an arduous journey if it seeks to impregnate the minds of strangers. The reward is that the time they spend experiencing the world you've created, will shape their consciousness every bit as tangibly as the time they spend at their boring jobs. With any luck, your work will have an even greater impact than many of their 'real-life' experiences. This is magic. This is expressing the divinity that lies dormant at the center of your being. The primary attribute humankind has always ascribed to God or gods is creativity.

My final word, therefore, is
Create.

"The syntactical nature of reality, the real secret of magic, is that the world is made of words.

And if you know the words that the world is made of, you can make of it whatever you wish."

- Terence McKenna

Lovecraft Tales Analysed

Ramsey Campbell

The fathers of the modern horror story are Poe in America and Le Fanu in Britain, both of whom refined Gothic methods to produce seminal stories in the field. Nor should Hoffman's psychological fantasies be overlooked. If I take Lovecraft to be the most important single twentieth-century writer of tales of terror, it's because he unites the traditions that preceded him on both sides of the Atlantic and builds on their strengths. His *Supernatural Horror in Literature* is not only an appreciation of all that he found best in the genre and a critique of the flaws he saw, but also a statement of his own artistic ambitions. His fiction gives them life.

To an extent his reputation is the victim of his most famous creation, the Lovecraft Mythos. This took very gradual shape throughout most of his career, and involves inhuman beings from outer space or from other dimensions, creatures that are indifferent to man but often worshipped as gods or occult forces. He often cited references to them from the *Necronomicon*, his invented tome that took on such a life of its own that several versions by later writers have been published. The Mythos was conceived as an antidote to conventional Victorian occultism – as an attempt to reclaim the imaginative appeal of the unknown – and is only one of many ways his tales suggest worse, or greater, than they show. It is also just one of his means of reaching for a sense of wonder, the aim that produces the visionary horror of his finest work (by no means all of it belonging to the Mythos). His stories represent a search for the perfect form for the weird tale, a process in which he tried out all the forms and all the styles of prose he could.

Nevertheless the Mythos is his most visible bequest to the field, because it looks so easy to imitate or draw upon. As one of the first writers to copy Lovecraft without having known him, I must take some of the blame for the way his concept has been rendered over-explicit and over-explained, precisely the reverse of his intentions. Luckily his influence is far more profound. In his essays and letters he was able to preserve the notion of horror fiction as literature despite all the assaults pulp writing had made on its best qualities, a view that was especially fruitful in the case of Fritz Leiber, who followed his mentor's example of uniting the transatlantic traditions. Other correspondents such as Robert Bloch, Donald Wandrei and Henry Kuttner assimilated his vision into their own. More recently such diverse talents as T. E. D. Klein, Thomas Ligotti and Poppy Z. Brite have acknowledged Lovecraft's importance to their work, but who could accuse any of them of simple mimicry? His use of suggestion and allusion might seem beyond the reach of most filmmakers, but I submit *The Blair Witch Project* as the key Lovecraftian film, not least in the documentary realism he urged upon serious artists in

the field and in the inexplicitness with which it conveys, to use his phrase, dread suspense.

Yet Lovecraft's achievement lies not so much in his influence as in the enduring qualities of his finest work. The field would be all the richer if more writers learned from both his care for structure and his larger principles. His yearning for the cosmic is the greatest strength of his best tales. He is one of the few masters of the tale of terror that reaches for, and often attains, awe. I'm going to examine in some detail the structures and use of language that he employed to this and other ends.

I want to start by looking at his earliest recognisably personal story, "Dagon". This was written in July 1917, and applies the principles he admired in Poe's tales of supernatural horror: "the maintenance of a single mood and achievement of a single impression in a tale, and the rigorous paring down of incidents to such as have a direct bearing on the plot and will figure prominently in the climax." Lovecraft wrote this in *Supernatural Horror in Literature*, where he analyses Poe's "The Fall of the House of Usher" as "demonstrating the essential details to emphasise, the precise incongruities and conceits to select as preliminaries or concomitants to horror, the exact incidents and allusions to throw out innocently in advance as symbols or prefigurings of each major step toward the hideous dénouement to come, the nice adjustments of cumulative force and the unerring accuracy in linkage of parts which make for faultless unity throughout and thunderous effectiveness at the climactic moment, the delicate nuances of scenic and landscape value to select in establishing and sustaining the desired mood and vitalising the desired illusion." It's worth remarking that when a writer analyses someone else's work they are often also talking about their own, and we shall see how he developed these methods in his own fiction.

August Derleth – prime mover of Arkham House, Lovecraft's first hardcover publisher – once summed up Lovecraft's structure thus: "Lovecraft got his effects by beginning soberly and with restraint, being careful to link his stories to reality, and proceeded with them with an air of doubt, as if the facts he chronicled could not mean what they did, so that the ultimate effect was all the more damning…." We may observe that the opening tone is often restrained even when the material is Gothic; like Poe, Lovecraft was refining elements of the Gothic novel, focusing more closely on psychology and the supernatural. So "Dagon" opens with the lines "I am writing this under an appreciable mental strain, since by tonight I shall be no more. Penniless, and at the end of my supply of the drug which alone makes life endurable, I can bear the torture no longer; and shall cast myself from this garret window into the squalid street below." While this is undoubtedly melodramatic, it serves to warn the reader to examine the narrator's tale carefully, since it may be some extent delusional. The unreliable narrator is a favourite and certainly effective device of the genre, enriching many tales since Poe's "Tell-tale Heart" with ambiguity. It often means that the tale can be interpreted psychologically without losing its uncanny dimension. Sometimes (as in *Rosemary's Baby*, which can certainly be read as a study of prenatal paranoia) restricting the reader's view to a single consciousness works just as well.

Having established the background to the narrator's situation in just three paragraphs, Lovecraft immediately immerses us in it. "The change happened while I slept…" Like quite a few of his stories, "Dagon" is based on a nightmare and seems designed to convey the intensity of that experience. The sense of dislocation – of finding yourself somewhere you have no memory of reaching – will recur in later tales; it's surely a powerful symbol of psychological breakdown. The paragraphs describing the upheaved landscape recall the opening of Poe's "Usher" (itself an object lesson in setting the scene) in their oppressive vividness. Besides painting the scene in words, Lovecraft uses sound (or rather its absence) and smell to render it more immediate. There's also an early use of a technique that his detractors often seize upon – inexplicitness as a means of stimulating the reader's imagination. Here the reference to "other less describable things" that infest the mud is surely appropriate, implying that they're the remains of creatures carried up from depths so profound that the narrator can't identify the species (which a later reference suggests is prehistoric). At the same time the phrase seems intended to evoke disquiet, and it works that way for me.

The paragraphs describing the narrator's trek and its destination exemplify a style of prose Lovecraft often writes: realistic in detail – documentary, if you like – and yet incantatory in its choice of language. At times the language rises to a crescendo that includes poetic usages ("I know not why my dreams were so wild that night; but ere the waning and fantastically gibbous moon had risen far above the eastern plain, I was awake in a cold perspiration, determined to sleep no more") but just as important to its effect are the modulations that lead up to the linguistic climaxes, best represented by the paragraph that describes the pictorial carvings on the monolith. A rare lurch into cliché ("Then suddenly I saw it") betrays that this is an early tale. The story ends with what can only be a hallucination, which throws the rest of the narrative into question but doesn't, I think, lessen the power of its vision. That this vision meant a good deal to Lovecraft is clear from its recurrence and elaboration in his later work.

When writing horror it's important to be aware of the difference between this genre and that of magic realism. In

"Notes on Writing Weird Fiction" (1937) Lovecraft writes "Never have a wonder taken for granted. Even when the characters are supposed to be accustomed to the wonder I try to weave an air of awe and impressiveness corresponding to what the reader should feel... Atmosphere, not action, is the great desideratum of weird fiction. Indeed, all that a wonder story can ever be is *a vivid picture of a certain type of human mood.*"

It's worth noting that in "Dagon" the narrator is entirely uncharacterised except by his behaviour; we never even learn what he was doing on the ship that was captured. There need be nothing wrong with this. Writers as different as Poe, Kafka and Samuel Beckett have conveyed terror by describing only a narrator's experiences, using them to illuminate his psychology. The American writer Steve Rasnic Tem has observed that the protagonist in a third-person tale of terror tends to be represented by a pronoun once they have been identified by name, so that they don't intervene too much between the narrative and our reading of their direct experience. In his essay "One View: Creating Character in Fantasy and Horror Fiction" he writes "all other objects in the story—the landscape, the other characters, the supernatural presence, even the individual events—represent some aspect of the protagonist (or victim)."

In "The Rats in the Walls" (written in August-September 1923) Lovecraft applies his documentary method to character, although the opening paragraphs are equally a chronicle of the location and an account of the tales told about it. By conflating these and the ancestry of the narrator he suggests how (again echoing Poe's "Usher") the place and its inhabitants share a common occult identity. It's also worth noting that the very first phrase establishes that the tale is set in what was then the present, adding to its immediacy. While effective tales of terror can still be set in the past – Susan Hill's *The Woman in Black*, for instance – modern work in the genre tends to use contemporary settings. Even if they've now been overtaken by nostalgia, writers such as M. R. James did at the time.

The narrator of "The Rats in the Walls" is de la Poer, the surname of a branch of Poe's ancestry. He's "a stolid Yankee" who has "merged into the greyness of Massachusetts business life". This justifies the sobriety of his narrative, but you may object that he hardly lives and breathes as a character; he isn't even allowed a first name. Even Lovecraft's most ardent admirers will admit that characterisation wasn't among his great strengths, but he developed a method that made this unnecessary, focusing on other aspects of the material. All the same, I'd argue that our narrator here is to some extent characterised by what he doesn't say. He expresses no grief over losing his injured son, and never even refers to the (deceased? estranged?) mother except to note her absence; we may conclude that he represses his emotions. Many manuals of composition recommend that writers should nurture every possible narrative skill; Stephen King's *On Writing* is a fine guide and more than that too – but you may also want to consider to what extent these skills enable you to convey and deal with your themes. Creative abilities aren't worth much if they're mechanically cultivated rather than growing organically out of the material.

The paragraphs that take us to Exham Priory maintain a light tone, the better to darken it later. The narrator's son is amused by the legends of the place, which is playfully portrayed as being "perched perilously upon a precipice", the kind of alliteration Lovecraft's apprentice Robert Bloch (later to write *Psycho* along with much else) would make central to his witty style. The son's friend Edward Norrys, who will become crucial to the tale, is said to be "a plump, amiable young man". One word in that phrase will come back to haunt the narrative, and planting this kind of almost subliminal hint can be a powerful device. The apparently superstitious villagers – not a cliché in themselves when "The Rats in the Walls" was written – regard the priory as "a haunt of fiends and werewolves". The hackneyed image both preserves the sense of rational disbelief that the accumulation of telling detail gradually undermines and prepares the way for darker revelations.

The mass of details in the next few paragraphs is artfully modulated; the subdued chronicle of the history of Exham is interspersed with hints about the family, which grow more evocative and sinister as they advance from indefinite "fireside tales" to ballads that seem disturbingly specific, and then to tales that Lovecraft makes the narrator call "hackneyed spectral lore". In fact not all of them are hackneyed, so that the phrase serves to emphasise their vivid strangeness and, in retrospect, their accuracy. It's surely a measure of Lovecraft's restraint that we are almost a third of the way through the story before he introduces the first reference to the rats of the title. The sober chronicle of the ancestor who fled to America is just ominous enough to foreshadow later events.

Having established the background, the story starts to build up telling details in the present. Note how the pet cat's restlessness is described as trite – again, a way of delaying acceptance of its significance. Similarly, the cat's later behaviour and that of its companions is presented as "picturesque" and accompanied by painterly images of architecture and lighting. By contrast, the narrator wakes into darkness from a nightmare rooted in the history of the place, and light shows him the first physical sign of the presence of the rats – or does it? Since nobody else has heard them, they could be a hallucination or proof that his senses are becoming bound up with his heritage.

As he and Norrys explore the sub-cellar they discover evidence of increasingly ancient practices; Lovecraft often uses such a progression to powerful effect. The two men keep a vigil in the cellar, and the narrator suffers a second nightmare whose climax and later significance is subtly hinted at: "…as I looked at these things they seemed nearer and more distinct—so distinct that I could almost observe their features. Then I did observe the flabby features of one of them—and awaked with such a scream that (…) Capt. Norrys, who had not slept, laughed considerably. Norrys might have laughed more—or perhaps less—had he known what it was that made me scream…" The alert reader may also note that Norrys is also described as "stouter" than his companion – another virtually subliminal detail that takes on a retrospective significance. During their vigil they learn that there is a vault below the sub-cellar. A progressive descent that reveals levels of new mystery is central to other Lovecraft tales – "The Mound" and "The Shadow out of Time", for instance.

Before the two men and a scientific party open the vault, the narrator has a third dream that sheds a sinister light on its predecessors without making the horror explicit. Lovecraft often allows the reader to anticipate on behalf of the protagonist, a method that can work just as well in horror as in tragedy, though it needs to be skilfully managed. Among the initial revelations is evidence that the passage to the vault was constructed from beneath the sub-cellar, a potently suggestive detail that's never explained. Does it imply that the de la Poer line was infiltrated by a subterranean race? In its inexplicability it helps the vault symbolise the narrator's subconscious – perhaps a hereditary one. At the sight of the contents of the vault Norrys appears to the narrator as "plump… utterly white and flabby" while de la Poer himself utters inarticulate sounds, images that prefigure the climax. Even now, despite the occasional rhetorical outburst – "Not Hoffmann or Huysmans could conceive a scene more wildly incredible, more frenetically repellent, or more Gothically grotesque than the twilit grotto through which we seven staggered" – most of the prose keeps its composure; that is, the narrator apparently keeps his. It's only when he ventures into the unlit gulf beneath the vault that he and his language regress, reverting like the layers of history through which the exploration has led him and fulfilling his identification with his house.

The reversion is preceded by several lines of the kind of prose that is popularly identified as Lovecraftian. "Then there came a sound from that inky, boundless, farther distance that I thought I knew; and I saw my old black cat dart past me like a winged Egyptian god, straight into the illimitable gulf of the unknown. But I was not far behind, for there was no doubt after another second. It was the eldritch scurrying of those fiend-born rats, always questing for new horrors, and determined to lead me on even unto those grinning caverns of earth's centre where Nyarlathotep, the mad faceless god, howls blindly to the piping of two amorphous idiot flute-players." I hope I've shown how carefully the culminating image here is prepared for, even within the paragraph; we may take the two Egyptian references as hinting at an occult correspondence between the horrors under Exham and ancient practices or legends elsewhere. In the dark he collides with "something soft and plump", and the reader hardly needs the final paragraph to confirm what the narrator refuses to admit. The final line rises to a crescendo as lyrical as it is horrific, and preserves the ambiguity of the narrative without lessening its cumulative power. It's as though all the narrator's repressions burst forth in the last few paragraphs, overtaking even his language before he regains some imperfect control.

The entire tale was "suggested by a very commonplace incident – the cracking of wallpaper late at night, and the chain of imaginings resulting from it." Such are the ways of fiction writing, which can transform the initial idea out of all recognition. "The Call of Cthulhu" (written in August or September 1926) was based on a dream, and Lovecraft recorded an element of the plot as early as 1920: "Man visits museum of antiquities—asks that it accept a bas-relief *he has* just made—*old* and learned curator laughs & says he cannot accept anything so modern. Man says that

'dreams are older than brooding Egypt or the contemplative Sphinx or garden-girdled Babylonia'

& that he had fashioned the sculpture in his dreams. Curator bids him shew his product, and when he does so curator shews horror. Asks who the man may be. He tells modern name. 'No—*before that*' says curator. Man does not remember except in dreams. Then curator offers high price, but man fears he means to destroy sculpture. Asks fabulous price—curator will consult directors. Add good development and describe nature of bas-relief."

Before considering the tale, let me note how important the opening lines are to the effect of many of his stories (while the final line of each is crucial, but to be appreciated in context rather than quoted here). Here are a few of the openings:

"Cautious investigators will hesitate to challenge the common belief that Robert Blake was killed by lightning, or by some profound nervous shock derived from an electrical discharge" ("The Haunter of the Dark")

"You ask me to explain why I am afraid of a draught of cool air; why I shiver more than others upon entering a cold room, and seem nauseated and repelled when the chill of evening creeps through the heat of a mild autumn day" ("Cool Air")

"Bear in mind closely that I did not see any actual visual horror at the end" ("The Whisperer in Darkness")

"It is true that I have sent six bullets through the head of my best friend, and yet I hope to shew by this statement that I am not his murderer" ("The Thing on the Doorstep")

"I am forced into speech because men of science have refused to follow my advice without knowing why" (*At the Mountains of Madness*)

"From a private hospital for the insane near Providence, Rhode Island, there recently disappeared an exceedingly singular person" (*The Case of Charles Dexter Ward*)

"From even the greatest of horrors irony is seldom absent" ("The Shunned House")

Other tales begin by setting the geographical scene; we'll see this in "The Colour out of Space". As for "The Call of Cthulhu", it's one of those that begin with a statement of an aspect of Lovecraft's philosophy: "The most merciful thing in the world, I think, is the inability of the human mind to correlate all its contents." Mating science fiction and the occult, the tale is his first sustained essay in cosmic terror, founded in his sense of the indifference of the universe and of man's insignificance in space and time. Perhaps it's the scale of his theme that prompts him to make the narrative more persuasive by assembling documents that lead inexorably to the vast truth. The structure had already been used to lend conviction to fantastic and macabre tales; Wilkie Collins employed it in *The Moonstone*, and Stoker did in *Dracula*. While Lovecraft may have learned from at least the latter novel, the probable primary influence is Arthur Machen, who constructs "The Great God Pan" along those lines (and who is referred to by name in the second chapter of Lovecraft's story). In "The Call of Cthulhu" the method bears out the ominous vision of the opening paragraph.

Amid the sobriety of the first pages there are hints of menace, carefully restrained. The cause of Professor Angell's death is barely touched upon, but the reader is expected to pick it up. The nature of the bas-relief is lightly sketched to be developed later, though even so early there's a suggestion of wrongness. All the Providence and New Orleans locations are real, as is the earthquake, adding verisimilitude. The sculptor Wilcox's words to the professor are virtually identical to those Lovecraft told his correspondents that he spoke in his own original dream (one of the few details that figure unchanged in the tale). Given his wild dreams, the sculptor may seem to be a questionable witness of anything real, and the narrative withholds any endorsement of his account except by mentioning the professor's unusual interest in it. Lovecraft is reining his effects back, the better to release them where they'll be most telling, but he does include a hint of the size of the subject of Wilcox's dream. When the narrator begins to be swayed by the similarity of numerous other accounts, he's still inclined to blame some bias in the collection or interpretation of the data. By now, however, we're made to feel his skepticism may be unreasonable. It's an effective method of winning the reader over when used with skill, as here.

The second section of the narrative reveals the reasons for Angell's obsession, all the more effectively for their having been delayed. It begins with a detailed description of the monster Wilcox sculpted. Even here, however, it's a sculpture that's described, which prefigures the eventual manifestation and allows Lovecraft not to go into such detail at the climax. I believe he may have learned this approach from M. R. James's ghost story "Canon Alberic's Scrapbook", which Lovecraft had read in late 1925 and which uses the same technique; James also favoured complex structures, sometimes non-chronological, to achieve his effects. Early in this chapter Angell cites a further set of similarities, but these are more difficult to dismiss than the dreams, since they're authenticated by experts. Still, at this point they can be viewed merely as legends, the stuff of anthropology. Even the police inspector's account of the Louisiana ritual is challenged in a sense: the beliefs of the cultists are said to indicate "an astonishing degree of cosmic imagination" although they "might be least expected to possess it", a sentence in which skepticism is brought to bear and then subtly undermined.

It's worth examining the tone of Inspector Legrasse's account as given by the narrator. While the cult and its behaviour, together with the location, are described in evocative language, I don't think we're invited to assume that these are necessarily the policeman's words. (In "The Space-Eaters", an early and intermittently very effective example of Lovecraft's influence, Lovecraft's friend Frank Belknap Long makes a policeman use this sort of language in direct speech, inadvertently undermining the credibility of the characterisation.) As a contrast, the paragraphs setting out the cult's beliefs are in plain prose – more accurately, a naïve voice, an effective method of conveying more than it openly states (a child's voice can be especially powerful). The quotation from the *Necronomicon* – the forbidden book that is one of Lovecraft's most famous inventions – recalls a verse from his minor 1920 tale "Polaris", lines that refer to the Pole Star:

"Slumber, watcher, till the spheres
Six and twenty thousand years
Have revolv'd, and I return
To the spot where now I burn...
Only when my round is o'er
Shall the past disturb thy door."

"The Call of Cthulhu" develops this in terms of cosmic terror. I said earlier that his mythos was designed as an antidote to Victorian occultism, which he saw as excessively conventionalised and organised. Both the mythos and the *Necronomicon* were intended as partial glimpses of larger imaginative vistas, and it's regrettable that so many writers have sought to codify them.

The narrator's skeptical tone persists even in his visit to the sculptor Wilcox, but he can't entirely keep it up, given that he's aware of more than he has told us so far. As in "The Rats in the Walls", the tone is invaded by expressions of repressed material. The final chapter starts by introducing the first document to be quoted in full, the newspaper clipping. While the report exemplifies reticence, a couple of suggestive phrases lie low amid the sober journalism. The last and most damning item, the Norwegian sailor's reminiscence, is paraphrased, which allows Lovecraft to modulate the language, so that the circumstantial detail of the opening sentences soon gives way to lyrical evocations of terror. Some of the descriptions of the island strongly recall "Dagon", but in terms of the vision Lovecraft has now developed and expanded.

There's also a recurrence of one of his most potent effects – the vista or object that despite its ability to disturb only hints at greater and more terrible secrets hidden beyond or beneath. I'd suggest that part of the power of this image derives, as in "The Rats in the Walls", from symbolising the unconscious; in "The Call of Cthulhu", of course, it's actually the source of dreams. I should add that there's no need for Lovecraft to have intended the symbolism; sometimes in fiction the most eloquent material is partly unconscious, an unintended effect of telling the tale. The mythic echoes in the revelation of the monster are more conscious – certainly the references to the Cyclops, and the lethal effect of looking back is an equally resonant image from myth. The reference to an occurrence "that the chronicler would not put on paper" may seem typically

Lovecraftian, but it has its origins in Kipling, who uses the technique twice in his horror story "The Mark of the Beast". Like "The Rats in the Walls", the present tale eventually but briefly bursts into delirious prose – "There is a sense of spectral whirling through liquid gulfs of infinity, of dizzying rides through reeling universes on a comet's tail, and of hysterical plunges from the pit to the moon and from the moon back again to the pit, all livened by a cachinnating chorus of the distorted, hilarious elder gods and the green, bat-winged mocking imps of Tartarus" – which is indeed a dream or a delirium. The last paragraphs do their best to recapture control, first in Johansen's coda and then the narrator's, but this can't overcome the cumulative effect of the tale, which may be said to employ conspiracy paranoia before the tendency became fashionable.

"The Colour out of Space" (written in March 1927) continues the evolution of Lovecraft's tales of terror towards science fiction. Later stories – "At the Mountains of Madness", "The Whisperer in Darkness", "The Shadow out of Time" – take this further, but in "Colour" he finds his single purest symbol of the otherness of the universe.

Hints of strangeness are woven into even the topographical realism of the opening paragraphs. The reference to "the hidden lore of old ocean, and all the mystery of primal earth" may resonate with readers of Lovecraft's earlier tales, but the images are delicate enough not to breach the understatement of the prose at this stage of the narrative. One way in which the scene-setting delays the full effect of the location is by holding it at a kind of aesthetic distance, with a theatrical reference ("the blasted heath") and a painterly one to Salvator Rosa. Just the same, there's a pronounced impression of wrongness, and the repetition of "the blasted heath" is followed by a description that reinvents the image. (As S. T. Joshi has pointed out, the phrase is both theatrical and poetic, having been used by Milton as well as Shakespeare.) The paragraph includes two images that will gather significance later: the "yawning black maw of an abandoned well whose stagnant vapours played strange tricks with the hues of the sunlight" and, more subtly, the "odd timidity about the deep skyey voids above" with which the place infects the unnamed narrator.

Like "The Call of Cthulhu" and other Lovecraft tales, the main text of "The Colour out of Space" is a story paraphrased by the narrator, which helps Lovecraft to control the tone and gives the reader the option of suspecting, at least to begin with, that the narrator's reconstruction of events may be unreliable. The meteorite and its effects are initially described in simple but evocative language (indeed, evocative because simple), which is followed by several paragraphs of scientific analysis that don't dissipate the sense of strangeness. A crucial event – the releasing of part of the contents of the meteorite – is shown with such reticence it's almost comical: "it burst with a nervous little pop". Again, the unnatural destruction of the meteorite is presented in purely scientific and meteorological terms, but all these details are being amassed towards conveying unease without acknowledging any reason for it. It's a case of letting the reader suspect worse than has been put into the words.

The first stages of the influence of the alien presence are very lightly conveyed. Nahum Gardner finds his work more tiring than formerly and blames his age. Lovecraft constructs many of his paragraphs towards a climactic sentence – in this case muted in its effect, but elsewhere (as in the lyrical passages I've quoted earlier) closer to classical musical structure. The new crop of fruit shows an "unwonted gloss", recalling the appearance of the meteorite. The alien taint begins to transform the wildlife, and despite the scientific reasons, the effects and the descriptions of them are oddly reminiscent of passages in George Macdonald's *The Princess and the Goblin*, a Victorian fairy tale in which animals have been mutated by magical influences; Lovecraft's increasing use of science in his fiction doesn't expunge the occult and fantastic but often embraces them, drawing on the imaginative strengths of both. The scientists who conducted the initial investigations of the meteorite now rationalise the effects around the Gardner farm, but the reader may well know better, although when the tale was written this dichotomy (between rationalists and some macabre truth) was less familiar in the genre. Employed skilfully, it can still work, and decades later Nigel Kneale made witty use of it in *Quatermass and the Pit*, a highly Lovecraftian piece.

The next few paragraphs grow oppressive with ominous details, psychological as well as physical. The first overt hints of something supernatural – the trees that move in no wind – are buried in the midst of paragraphs rather than dramatically placed at the end. Lovecraft may have learned this technique of unobtrusiveness in the layout of the material from M. R. James, who often uses this to startling effect (beware a recently edited edition of James that breaks down the paragraphs into shorter sections). Even when madness overtakes the Gardner family the language stays resolutely sober, except in the fragments of the mother's ravings. The hideous death of a family member is described by analogy with an earlier event, a reticent approach that I think adds to the horror.

The central section of the tale gives up detachment at last, with the informant Ammi Pierce's visit to the Gardner farm. The language only very gradually mounts to a pitch of physical horror, meanwhile subtly consolidating the hints of conscious alien activity around the farm (though even this is deftly qualified by the line "a buggy-wheel must have brushed the coping and knocked in a stone", which we're free to take at face value if we like, but not for long). The language reaches a crescendo with the scene of Nahum's death, particularly his monologue. In *On Writing* Stephen King describes Lovecraft as "a genius when it came to tales of the macabre, but a terrible dialogue writer," and cites this monologue as proof. Is it, though, when taken in context? After all, it's a report by the narrator of what Ammi Pierce (described at the outset as "rambling" with a mind that has "snapped a trifle") recalled nearly fifty years later. I think Lovecraft uses it as a way of modulating the tone of the narrative rather than as literal dialogue. Stephen objects that it consists of "carefully constructed elliptical bursts of information", but it reminds me oddly of the gasping voices we find in Samuel Beckett's later plays and prose. I can also report that I've read the whole story aloud to an audience and made Nahum's monologue work perfectly well.

As soon as Pierce flees the Gardner farm the prose reverts to sobriety, preparing for the final climax. Having progressed through understatement to gruesomeness, the story will reach for awe ("wonder and terror", as Fritz Leiber puts it). Unadorned prose and a scrap of rustic dialogue – more properly, another monologue – give way to ornate evocative language as the manifestations become unambiguous. Even so, just as in the previous two stories I've looked at here, delirious images are kept to a single sentence: "It was a monstrous constellation of unnatural light, like a glutted swarm of corpse-fed fireflies dancing hellish sarabands over an accursed marsh." The later passage that describes the "riot of luminous amorphousness" performed by the colour recalls Mrs Gardner's ravings, since the language consists very largely of verbs – a way of preserving suggestiveness while offering vividness.

To what extent may Lovecraft have been aware how Freudian some of the images of the well are? In 1921 he commented "We may not like to accept Freud, but I fear we shall have to do so." I suspect he would have repudiated any sexual reading of the investigation of the well, simply because it detracts from the sense of awe and terror he wants to convey. Such readings can be useful if they enrich a text, and for some readers they may do here. The disturbance of the well begins the upsurge of language and imagery that is rounded off by an ominous diminuendo, Pierce's glimpse of a trace of the colour that returns to the well. Form and content are one throughout the whole climactic scene. The extended coda sinks into language that is mostly plain, but of course this has gained resonance from the entire narrative – even such an unemphatic phrase as "the splotch of grey dust". However, Lovecraft uses one extraordinary verbal trick, repeating word for word the narrator's sentence about his own timidity from the opening scene. Some of the final lines might almost be trying to reduce the significance of the alien visitation, but the tale is surely proof against that. "It was just a colour out of space", but it epitomises Lovecraft's vision at least as powerfully as his mythos.

Since his death in 1937 he has emerged as one of the most important writers in the field, and a pervasive influence. He both drew on the strengths of the authors he most admired – Poe, Algernon Blackwood (whose tale "The Willows", with its evocation of absolute alienness, Lovecraft regarded as the greatest in the field), Arthur Machen, with his melding of Victorian science and the occult, and his sense of fairy tales and legends as metaphors for darker truths – and sought to improve on their limitations, as Lovecraft saw them. His ability in his best work to suggest terrors larger than he shows is as important as his attention to the power of language. While he wasn't averse to conveying "loathsome fright", his most lasting legacy is the sense of mingled wonder and dread. His influence has been celebrated by a remarkable variety of writers; besides those I named at the outset, consider Alan Moore, Jorge Luis Borges, Stephen King, Thomas Pynchon, Mark Samuels, Caitlín Kiernan, China Miéville, Laird Barron… Artists as different as H. R. Giger and John Coulthart have drawn inspiration from him, and directors such as Roger Corman, Sean Branney and Stuart Gordon have filmed his tales. His importance as a writer has been recognised by both the Library of America and Penguin Modern Classics, and the Penguin editions offer definitive restored texts. May his positive qualities continue to enrich literature! Horror fiction is much the better for them.

Let me end with a list of further recommendations. These stories demonstrate the considerable range of his best shorter work:

"The Outsider" (1921). Reminiscent of Poe's prose poems but original and personal; quite possibly an unconscious autobiographical metaphor.

"The Music of Erich Zann" (December 1921). Musical prose expressing a musical theme.

"The Festival" (1923). A delirious yet controlled tale that descends into the concealed antecedents of Christianity, and the first of his stories to cite a passage from the *Necronomicon* as background.

"Pickman's Model" (1926). Narrated in a conversational style, and exemplifying the dark humour (in this case deriving from Ambrose Bierce) that often figures in his work.

"The Thing on the Doorstep" (21-24 August 1933). Lovecraft's possession tale, reaching back through personality after personality to the possibly inhuman. As in

"The Colour out of Space", there's an unemphasised poignancy about the characterisation and relationships.

"The Haunter of the Dark" (November 1935). Lovecraft's last major tale, suggested by an actual church in Providence and written as a wry tribute to his young correspondent Robert Bloch. A final melding of the occult and the astronomical, and an essay in the terrors of somnambulism.

Biographies

Jasper Bark is infectious—and there's no known cure. If you're reading this then you're already at risk of contamination. The symptoms will begin to manifest any moment now. There's nothing you can do about it. There's no itching or unfortunate rashes, but you'll become obsessed with his books, from the award winning collections *Dead Air* and *Stuck on You and Other Prime Cuts*, to cult novels like *The Final Cut* and acclaimed graphic novels such as *Bloodfellas* and *Beyond Lovecraft*.

Soon you'll want to tweet, post and blog about his work until thousands of others fall under its viral spell. We're afraid there's no way to avoid this, these words contain a power you are hopeless to resist. You're already in their thrall and have been since you began reading this bio. Even now you find yourself itching to read the whole of his work. Don't fight it, embrace the urge and wear your obsession with pride!

Kenneth W. Cain is the prolific author of *A Season in Hell*, *Darker Days*, *Embers*, and several other books, short stories, poems, and articles. He is also the editor of the well-known anthologies *Tales from The Lake Volume 5*, *When the Clock Strikes 13*, and *Midnight in the Graveyard*. As an Active member of the Horror Writers Association, he is chair for the membership committee, heads the Pennsylvania chapter, and was given the 2017 Silver Hammer Award for his service. Currently, Cain helps several publishers with their editing, formatting, book cover, and graphic design needs. Cain resides in Chester County, Pennsylvania with his wife and two children.

The *Oxford Companion to English Literature* describes **Ramsey Campbell** as "Britain's most respected living horror writer". He has been given more awards than any other writer in the field, including the Grand Master Award of the World Horror Convention, the Lifetime Achievement Award of the Horror Writers Association, the Living Legend Award of the International Horror Guild and the World Fantasy Lifetime Achievement Award. In 2015 he was made an Honorary Fellow of Liverpool John Moores University for outstanding services to literature. Among his novels are *The Face That Must Die, Incarnate, Midnight Sun, The Count of Eleven, Silent Children, The Darkest Part of the Woods, The Overnight, Secret Story, The Grin of the Dark, Thieving Fear, Creatures of the Pool, The Seven Days of Cain, Ghosts Know, The Kind Folk, Think Yourself Lucky, Thirteen Days by Sunset Beach* and *The Wise Friend*. He recently brought out his Brichester Mythos trilogy, consisting of *The Searching Dead, Born to the Dark* and *The Way of the Worm. Needing Ghosts, The Last Revelation of Gla'aki, The Pretence* and *The Booking* are novellas. His collections include *Waking Nightmares, Alone with the Horrors, Ghosts and Grisly Things, Told by the Dead, Just Behind You, Holes for Faces, By the Light of My Skull* and a two-volume retrospective roundup (*Phantasmagorical Stories*). His non-fiction is collected as *Ramsey Campbell, Probably* and *Ramsey's Rambles* (video reviews). *Limericks of the Alarming and Phantasmal* is a history of horror fiction in the form of fifty limericks. His novels *The Nameless, Pact of the Fathers* and *The Influence* have been filmed in Spain. He is the President of the Society of Fantastic Films.

Ramsey Campbell lives on Merseyside with his wife Jenny. His pleasures include classical music, good food and wine, and whatever's in that pipe. His web site is at www.ramseycampbell.com.

A former stage hypnotist, folksinger, and high school teacher, **Mort Castle** has been a publishing writer since 1967, with hundreds of stories, articles, comics and books published in a dozen languages. Castle has won three Bram Stoker Awards®, two Black Quill awards, the Golden Bot (*Wired Magazine*), and has been nominated for The Audie, The Shirley Jackson award, the International Horror Guild award and the Pushcart Prize. In 2000, the Chicago Sun-Times News Group cited him as one of Twenty-One "Leaders in the Arts for the 21st Century in Chicago's Southland." A feature film based on his novel *The Strangers* is currently in development by New Zealand's Light in the Dark Productions. Castle and his wife, Jane, have been married 48 years and live in Crete, Illinois.

Ben Eads lives within the semi-tropical suburbs of Central Florida. A true horror writer by heart, he wrote his first story at the tender age of ten. The look on the teacher's face when she read it was priceless. However, his classmates loved it! Ben's short fiction has appeared in magazines or anthologies by: Crystal Lake Publishing, Shroud Magazine, and Seventh Star Press. His first novella, *Cracked Sky*, was published in 2015 by the Bram Stoker Award® Winning press Omnium Gatherum. His latest book, *Hollow Heart*, will be published November 29th by Crystal Lake Publishing.
www.beneadsfiction.com
Facebook: https://www.facebook.com/ben.eads.58
https://twitter.com/Ben_Eads

David Owain Hughes is a word-slinger of horror and crime fiction, who grew up on trashy b-movies from the age of five which helped rapidly instill in him a vivid imagination. He's had multiple short stories published in various online magazines and anthologies, along with articles, reviews and interviews. He's written for *This Is Horror*, *Blood Magazine*, and *Horror Geeks Magazine*.

Hughes is the author of six horror novels, four short story collections, and a plethora of novellas. Although he predominately writes within the bracket of horror and its multiple sub-genres, he's recently branched out into crime fiction and is slowly carving out a superb series of crime/noir thrillers under the umbrella title of *South Wales*.

https://www.facebook.com/DOHughesAuthor
http://www.amazon.co.uk/David-Owain-Hughes/e/B00L708P2M
http://david-owain-hughes.wix.com/horrorwriter
https://www.goodreads.com/author/show/4877205.David_Owain_Hughes
https://twitter.com/DOHUGHES32

Stephen Graham Jones is the author of sixteen and a half novels, six story collections, a couple of standalone novellas, and a couple of one-shot comic books. Stephen's been an NEA recipient, has won the Texas Institute of Letters Award for Fiction, the Independent Publishers Award for Multicultural Fiction, a Bram Stoker Award©, four This is Horror Awards, and he's been a finalist for the Shirley Jackson Award and the World Fantasy Award. He's also made Bloody Disgusting's Top Ten Horror Novels, and is the guy who wrote *Mongrels*. Next up are *The Only Good Indians* (Saga) and *Night of the Mannequins* (Tor.com). Stephen lives in Boulder, Colorado.

Kevin J Kennedy is a horror author & editor from Scotland. He is the co-author of *You Only Get One Shot* &

Screechers and has two solo collections available called *Dark Thoughts* and *Vampiro and Other Strange Tales of the Macabre*. He is the publisher of several bestselling anthology series; *Collected Horror Shorts*, *100 Word Horrors* & *The Horror Collection*, as well as the stand-alone anthology *Carnival of Horror*. His stories have been featured in many other notable books in the horror genre.

He lives in a small town in Scotland, with his wife and his two little cats, Carlito and Ariel.

Keep up to date with new releases or contact Kevin through his website: www.kevinjkennedy.co.uk

From the day she was born, Bram Stoker Award© winner **Jess Landry** has always been attracted to the darker things in life. Her fondest childhood memories include getting nightmares from the *Goosebumps* books, watching *The Hilarious House of Frightenstein*, and reiterating to her parents that there was absolutely nothing wrong with her mental state.

Her fiction has appeared in anthologies such as *Twice-Told: A Collection of Doubles*, *Monsters of Any Kind*, *Where Nightmares Come From, Lost Highways: Dark Fictions from the Road*, and *Fantastic Tales of Terror*, and her debut feature screenplay, *My Only Sunshine*, is currently being shopped.

You can find her online at jesslandry.com or on Facebook and Twitter (@jesslandry28) where she often posts cat gifs and references *Jurassic Park* way too much.

Kevin Lucia is the Reviews Editor for Cemetery Dance Magazine. His column "Revelations" is featured on Cemetery Dance Online. His short fiction has appeared in several anthologies, most recently with Neil Gaiman, Clive Barker, Bentley Little, Peter Straub and Robert McCammon.

His first short story collection, *Things Slip Through* was published November 2013, followed by *Devourer of Souls* in June 2014, *Through A Mirror, Darkly*, June 2015, and his second short story collection, *Things You Need*, September 2018. His limited edition novella *Mystery Road* is available for order from Cemetery Dance Publications.

Chad Lutzke has written for *Famous Monsters of Filmland*, *Rue Morgue*, *Cemetery Dance*, and *Scream* magazine. He's had a few dozen short stories published, and some of his books include: *Of Foster Homes & Flies*, *Wallflower*, *Stirring the Sheets*, *Skullface Boy*, *The Same Deep Water as You*, and *The Pale White*. Lutzke's work has been praised by authors Jack Ketchum, Stephen Graham Jones, James Newman, Elizabeth Massie, *Cemetery Dance*, and his own mother. He can be found lurking the internet at www.chadlutzke.com.

Bret McCormick is a writer, artist and filmmaker based in Bedford, Texas. From 1984 to 1996 he was the most prolific producer/director of independent feature films working in the state of Texas. His ultra-low-budget horror film *The Abomination* (1986) maintains a small, but dedicated cult following internationally. McCormick has edited or co-edited five anthologies of horror fiction including, in 2019, *Road Kill Volume 4* and *The Toilet Zone* published by HellBound Books. His nonfiction title *Texas Schlock*: *B-Movie Sci-Fi and Horror from the Lone Star State* is a favorite of film geeks everywhere. His most recent publication is the novel *Skin Dreams (Poor White Trash Part 3),* also from HellBound Books. McCormick is employed by the Bedford Public Library and volunteers five days a week with the After School Art Program at

Central Arts of Hurst, Texas. He can be reached at texaswriterman2014@gmail.com.

Joe Mynhardt is a Bram Stoker Award-winning South African publisher, editor, and mentor.

A former primary school teacher, Joe is now the owner and CEO of Crystal Lake Publishing, which he founded in August, 2012. Since then he's published and edited short stories, novellas, interviews and essays by the likes of Neil Gaiman, Clive Barker, Stephen King, Charlaine Harris, Ramsey Campbell, John Connolly, Jack Ketchum, Jonathan Maberry, Christopher Golden, Graham Masterton, Damien Angelica Walters, Adam Nevill, Lisa Morton, Elizabeth Massie, Josh Malerman, Joe R. Lansdale, Edward Lee, Paul Tremblay, Wes Craven, John Carpenter, George A. Romero, Mick Garris, and hundreds more. Yes, hundreds.

Just like Crystal Lake Publishing, which strives to be a platform for launching author careers, Joe believes in reaching out to all authors, new and experienced, and being a beacon of friendship and guidance in the Dark Fiction field.

You can read more about Joe and Crystal Lake Publishing at www.crystallakepub.com or find him on Facebook.

Lisa Morton is a screenwriter, author of non-fiction books, and award-winning prose writer whose work was described by the American Library Association's *Readers' Advisory Guide to Horror* as "consistently dark, unsettling, and frightening". She is the author of four novels and 150 short stories, a six-time winner of the Bram Stoker Award®, and a world-class Halloween expert. Her most recent book, *Ghost Stories: Classic Tales of Horror and Suspense* (co-edited with Leslie Klinger) received a starred review in *Publishers Weekly*, who called it "a work of art";

forthcoming in 2020 is *Calling the Spirits: A History of Seances*. Lisa lives in the San Fernando Valley and online at www.lisamorton.com.
Website: http://www.lisamorton.com
Facebook: https://www.facebook.com/lisa.morton.165
Twitter: https://twitter.com/cinriter

Scott Nicholson is author of more than 30 books, including the After, Next, and Arize post-apocalyptic series. His novel *The Red Church* was a Stoker Award finalist. He lives in the Blue Ridge Mountains of North Carolina.

Gene O'Neill has seen about 200 of his stories and novellas published, several reprinted in France, Spain, and Russia. Some of these stories have been collected in *Ghost Spirits*, *Computers & World Machines*, *The Grand Struggle*, *In Dark Corners*, *Dance of the Blue Lady*, *The Hitchhiking Effect*, *Lethal Birds*, and *Frozen Shadows and Other Chilling Stories*. He has seen six novels published. Gene has been a Stoker finalist twelve times. In 2010 *Taste of Tenderloin* won the haunted house for Collection; in 2012 *The Blue Heron* won for Long Fiction. A series of two novels in The White Plague Chronicles will come out in 2020—The *Sarawak Virus* in the winter, *Beyond Pandemic* soon after. Also out in 2020, *Entangled Soul*, a collaborative novella, with Chris Marrs. Recently, he finished and turned in *A Stick of Doublemint*, the fourth book in ther katy Green Crime Files series.

He is currently working on a novel with Gord Rollo.

Gene lives in the Napa Valley with his wife, Kay. He has two grown children, Gavin, who lives in Oakland, and Kaydee who lives in Carlsbad and rides herd on his two g-kids, Fiona and TJ. When he isn't writing or visiting g-kids, Gene likes to read good fiction or watch sports—all of them, especially boxing.

Marie O'Regan is a three-time British Fantasy Award-nominated author and editor, based in Derbyshire. Her first collection, *Mirror Mere*, was published in 2006 by Rainfall Books; her second, *In Times of Want*, came out in September 2016 from Hersham Horror Books. Her third, *The Last Ghost and Other Stories*, was published by Luna Press early in 2019. Her short fiction has appeared in a number of genre magazines and anthologies in the UK, US, Canada, Italy and Germany, including *Best British Horror 2014*, *Great British Horror: Dark Satanic Mills* (2017), and *The Mammoth Book of Halloween Stories*. Her novella, *Bury Them Deep*, was published by Hersham Horror Books in September 2017. She was shortlisted for the British Fantasy Society Award for Best Short Story in 2006, and Best Anthology in 2010 (*Hellbound Hearts*) and 2012 (*Mammoth Book of Ghost Stories by Women*). Her genre journalism has appeared in magazines like *The Dark Side*, *Rue Morgue* and *Fortean Times*, and her interview book with prominent figures from the horror genre, *Voices in the Dark*, was released in 2011. An essay on 'The Changeling' was published in PS Publishing's *Cinema Macabre*, edited by Mark Morris. She is co-editor of the bestselling *Hellbound Hearts*, *Mammoth Book of Body Horror*, *A Carnivàle of Horror–Dark Tales from the Fairground*, *Exit Wounds* and *Wonderland*, plus editor of bestselling *The Mammoth Book of Ghost Stories by Women* and *Phantoms*. She is Co-Chair of the UK Chapter of the Horror Writers' Association, and is currently organising StokerCon UK, which will take place in Scarborough in April 2020. Marie is represented by Jamie Cowen of The Ampersand Agency.

Kelli Owen is the author of more than a dozen books, including the novels *Teeth* and *Floaters*, and novellas *Wilted Lilies* and *Waiting Out Winter*. Her fiction spans the genres from thrillers to psychological horror, with an occasional bloodbath, and an even rarer happy ending. She was an editor and reviewer for over a decade, and has attended countless writing conventions, participated on dozens of panels, and spoken at the CIA Headquarters in Langley, VA regarding both her writing and the field in general. Visit her website at kelliowen.com for more information.

Author **John Palisano** has a pair of books with Samhain Publishing, *Dust of The Dead*, and *Ghost Heart*. *Nerves* is available through Bad Moon. *Starlight Drive: Four Halloween Tales* was released in time for Halloween, and his first short fiction collection *All That Withers* is available from Cycatrix press, celebrating over a decade of short story highlights. *Night of 1,000 Beasts* is also now available.

He won the Bram Stoker Award© in short fiction in 2016 for "Happy Joe's Rest Stop." More short stories have appeared in anthologies from Cemetery Dance, Space & Time, PS Publishing, Independent Legions, DarkFuse, Crystal Lake, Terror Tales, Lovecraft eZine, Horror Library, Bizarro Pulp, Written Backwards, Dark Continents, Big Time Books, McFarland Press, Darkscribe, Dark House, Omnium Gatherum, and more.

Non-fiction pieces have appeared in Blumhouse, Fangoria, Backstreets and Dark Discoveries magazines.

He is currently serving as the President of the Horror Writers Association.

Say 'hi' at: www.johnpalisano.com
and http://www.amazon.com/author/johnpalisano
and www.facebook.com/johnpalisano
and www.twitter.com/johnpalisano

Armand Rosamilia runs two podcasts, Arm Cast Podcast (where he will hopefully interview you in the future) and The Mando Method Podcast with co-host Chuck Buda (where he talks about writing, publishing and answers listener questions).

He loves podcasting so much he also owns the group they're on, Project Entertainment Network, with over a dozen quality podcasts for your listening pleasure.

And he'd love to be interviewed on your podcast, too! Practice what you preach and all that jazz.

Lucy A. Snyder is the Shirley Jackson Award-nominated and five-time Bram Stoker Award-winning author of over 100 published short stories. Her most recent books are the collection *Garden of Eldritch Delights* and the forthcoming novel *The Girl With the Star-Stained Soul*. She also wrote the novels *Spellbent, Shotgun Sorceress*, and *Switchblade Goddess*, the nonfiction book *Shooting Yourself in the Head for Fun and Profit: A Writer's Survival Guide*, and the collections *While the Black Stars Burn, Soft Apocalypses, Orchid Carousals, Sparks and Shadows, Chimeric Machines,* and *Installing Linux on a Dead Badger*. Her writing has been translated into French, Russian, Italian, Spanish, Czech, and Japanese editions and has appeared in publications such as *Asimov's Science Fiction, Apex Magazine, Nightmare Magazine, Pseudopod, Strange Horizons,* and *Best Horror of the Year*. She lives in Columbus, Ohio and is faculty in Seton Hill University's MFA program in Writing Popular Fiction. You can learn more about her at www.lucysnyder.com and you can follow her on Twitter at @LucyASnyder.

Monique Snyman's mind is a confusing bedlam of glitter and death, where candy-coated gore is found in abundance and homicidal unicorns thrive. Sorting out the mess in her head is particularly irksome before she's ingested a specific amount of coffee, which is equal to half the recommended intake of water for humans per day. When she's not playing referee to her imaginary friends or trying to overdose on caffeine, she's doing something with words—be it writing, reading, or fixing all the words.

Monique Snyman lives in Pretoria, South Africa, with her husband and an adorable Chihuahua. She's the author of *Muti Nation*, a horror novel set in South Africa, and the Bram Stoker Award® nominated novel, *The Night Weaver*, which is the first installment in a dark fantasy series for young adults.

Steve Rasnic Tem's writing career spans over 40 years, including poetry, plays, short stories, and novels in the genres of fantasy, science fiction, horror, crime, regional fiction set in the Appalachian South, as well as a less-classifiable imaginative prose more than one critic has called "Temism." His collaborative novella with his late wife Melanie Tem, *The Man On The Ceiling*, won the World Fantasy, Bram Stoker, and International Horror Guild awards in 2001. He has also won the Bram Stoker, International Horror Guild, and British Fantasy Awards for his solo work. His recent novel *UBO* (Solaris, January 2017) is a dark science fictional tale about violence and its origins, featuring such historical viewpoint characters as Jack the Ripper, Stalin, and Heinrich Himmler. A handbook on fiction writing, *Yours to Tell: Dialogues on the Art & Practice of Fiction*, written with his late wife Melanie, appeared in 2017 from Apex Books.

Steve has published over 450 short stories. His most recent collections include *Figures Unseen: Selected Stories* (Valancourt, 2018), *The Harvest Child And Other Fantasies* (Crossroads, 2018), the YA-oriented *Everything Is Fine Now* (Omnium Gatherum, 2019), and *The Night*

Doctor and Other Tales (Centipede, 2019). A transplanted Southerner from Lee County Virginia, Steve is a long-time resident of Colorado. He has a BA in English Education from VPI and a MA in Creative Writing from Colorado State, where he studied fiction under Warren Fine and poetry under Bill Tremblay.

Visit his website at www.stevetem.com. His Facebook page is www.facebook.com/steve.tem

Richard Thomas is the award-winning author of seven books: three novels—*Disintegration* and *Breaker* (Penguin Random House Alibi), as well as *Transubstantiate* (Otherworld Publications); three short story collections—*Staring into the Abyss* (Kraken Press), *Herniated Roots* (Snubnose Press), and *Tribulations* (Cemetery Dance); and one novella in *The Soul Standard* (Dzanc Books). With over 150 stories published, his credits include *The Best Horror of the Year* (Volume Eleven), *Cemetery Dance* (twice), *Behold!: Oddities, Curiosities and Undefinable Wonders* (Bram Stoker winner), *PANK, storySouth, Gargoyle, Weird Fiction Review, Midwestern Gothic, Shallow Creek, The Seven Deadliest, Gutted: Beautiful Horror Stories, Qualia Nous, Chiral Mad* (numbers 2-4), *PRISMS, Pantheon,* and *Shivers VI* (with Stephen King and Peter Straub). He has won contests at ChiZine and One Buck Horror, has received five Pushcart Prize nominations, and has been long-listed for *Best Horror of the Year* six times. He was also the editor of four anthologies: *The New Black* and *Exigencies* (Dark House Press), *The Lineup: 20 Provocative Women Writers* (Black Lawrence Press) and *Burnt Tongues* (Medallion Press) with Chuck Palahniuk. He has been nominated for the Bram Stoker, Shirley Jackson, and Thriller awards. In his spare time he is a columnist at Lit Reactor. He was the Editor-in-Chief at Dark House Press and *Gamut Magazine*. His agent is Paula

Munier at Talcott Notch. For more information visit www.whatdoesnotkillme.com.

Tim Waggoner's first novel came out in 2001, and since then he's published close to fifty novels and seven collections of short stories. He writes original dark fantasy and horror, as well as media tie-ins. His novels include *Like Death*, considered a modern classic in the genre, and the popular Nekropolis series of urban fantasy novels. He's written tie-in fiction for *Supernatural, Grimm, the X-Files, Doctor Who, A Nightmare on Elm Street, Alien*, and *Transformers*, among others, and he's written novelizations for films such as *Kingsman: the Golden Circle* and *Resident Evil: the Final Chapter*. His articles on writing have appeared in *Writer's Digest, Writer's Journal, Writer's Workshop of Horror*, and *Where Nightmares Come From*. In 2017 he received the Bram Stoker Award for Superior Achievement in Long Fiction, and he's been a multiple finalist for the Shirley Jackson Award and the Scribe Award. His fiction has received numerous Honorable Mentions in volumes of *Best Horror of the Year*, and in 2016, the Horror Writers Association honored him with the Mentor of the Year Award. In addition to writing, he's also a full-time tenured professor who teaches creative writing and composition at Sinclair College.

Luke Walker has been writing horror, fantasy and dark thrillers for most of his life. The new novel *The Dead Room* is out now as are *The Day Of The New Gods, The Mirror Of The Nameless, The Unredeemed, Ascent, Hometown, Die Laughing* and *Dead Sun. Pandemonium* and *The Kindred* will be published by HellBound Books in 2019/20. Several of his short stories have been published online and in magazines/books. While writing, he has worked in a library, a hospital (disposing of severed legs) and a record shop (back in the distant past).

Luke welcomes comments at his blog which can be read at www.lukewalkerwriter.com and his Twitter page is @lukewalkerbooks. Sign up to his newsletter at www.tinyletter.com/LukeWalkerWriter

He is forty-two and lives in England with his wife, cats, too many bad films and not enough books.

Stephanie M. Wytovich is an American poet, novelist, and essayist. Her work has been showcased in numerous venues such as *Weird Tales*, *Gutted: Beautiful Horror Stories*, *Fantastic Tales of Terror*, *Year's Best Hardcore Horror: Volume 2*, *The Best Horror of the Year: Volume 8*, as well as many others.

Wytovich is the Poetry Editor for Raw Dog Screaming Press, an adjunct at Western Connecticut State University, Southern New Hampshire University, and Point Park University, and a mentor with Crystal Lake Publishing. She is a member of the Science Fiction Poetry Association, an active member of the Horror Writers Association, and a graduate of Seton Hill University's MFA program for Writing Popular Fiction. Her Bram Stoker Award-winning poetry collection, *Brothel*, earned a home with Raw Dog Screaming Press alongside *Hysteria: A Collection of Madness*, *Mourning Jewelry*, *An Exorcism of Angels*, *Sheet Music to My Acoustic Nightmare*, and most recently, *The Apocalyptic Mannequin*. Her debut novel, *The Eighth*, is published with Dark Regions Press.

Follow Wytovich on her blog at http://stephaniewytovich.blogspot.com/ and on twitter @SWytovich.

Other HellBound Books Titles
Available at: www.hellboundbookspublishing.com

Ghosts Spirits and Specters

Compiled and edited by the Dark Poet Princess herself - Xtina Marie - Ghosts, Spirits, & Specters boasts eighteen terrifying tales of ethereal and ghostly goings-on from the gloriously fevered minds of:

Michael J. Moore, T. Fox Dunham, Richard Raven, Sarah Cannavo, DJ Tyrer, Kev Harrison, David F. Gray, Jon O'Bergh, Dustin Chisam, Bill Davidson, Nathan Helton, Brian James Lewis, Trevor Newton, R.C. Mulhare, Nikki D. Freeman, Laszlo Tamasfi, Dawson Goodell, and Eric Nash

The Toilet Zone

RESTROOM READING AT ITS MOST FRIGHTENING!

Compiled and edited by the grand master of 80's schlock horror, Bret McCormick, each one of this collection of 32 terrifying tales is just the perfect length for a visit to the smallest room....

At the very boundaries of human imagination dwells one single, solitary place of solitude, of peace and quiet, a place in which your regular human being spends, on average, 10 to 15 minutes - at least once every single day of their lives.

Now, consider a typical, everyday reading speed of 200 to 250 words per minute - that means your average visitor has the time to read between 2,500 to 4,000 words, which makes each and every one of these 32 tales of terror - from some of the best contemporary independent authors - within this anthology of horror the perfect, meticulously calculated length. Dare you take a walk to the small room from where inky shadows creep out to smother the light and solitude's siren call beckons you?

Dare you take a quiet, lonely walk into… The Toilet Zone?

Road Kill 4: Texas Horror by Texas Writers

For four years now, Bret McCormick and E. R. Bills have been beating the bushes and peering into abandoned wells to seek out the most terrifying tales the Lone Star State has to offer. They have left no stone unturned, no attic unexplored, and no grave undesecrated.

And boy howdy, their diligence has paid off! Road Kill Volume 4 is the best and grimmest yet!

You hold in your hands a grand collection of 16 goose-flesh-inducing prose. But, don't just take our word for it; these sixteen stories speak – or perhaps scream – for themselves.

Featuring tales of Texas terror from:

Corey Lamb, E. R. Bills, James H Longmore, William Jensen, Patrick C. Harrison III, W. H. Gilbert, Jeremy Hepler, Dan Fields, Thomas Kearnes, Sylvia Ney , Mark A. Nobles, Russell C. Connor, Elliott Baxter, Ralph Robert Moore, Carmen Gray, and Andrew Kozma

An Unholy Trinity Volume 2

FOUR HORRIFYING NOVELLAS,
FOUR EXCEPTIONAL AUTHORS,
ALL IN ONE PHENOMENAL BOOK!

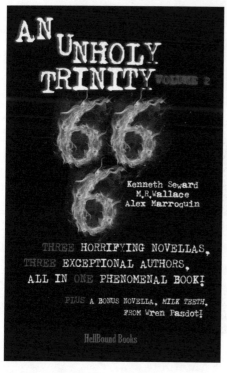

THE BLOODMOON EXPRESS - M.R. Wallace

Following a failed case in London three years before, Ian DeWitt finds himself on Le Train Bleu. The famous passenger train will ferry him to the warm shores of the Mediterranean for a much-needed rest. Ian soon finds that the horrors of the past have followed him, and the resplendent luxury train becomes the hunting ground for a monster all too familiar to the beleaguered Scotland Yard detective. Running out of time and woefully unequipped to combat such a beast, DeWitt must discover the identity of the creature and attempt to stop it before they are torn to shreds.

SAVAGES FOR REVENGE - Alex Marroquin

Failing as an artist, Derrick de Sousa travels to Argentina to recover his artistic inspiration after his college sweetheart invites him to reunite with her at Buenos Aires. Instead, he finds himself forced into a path of murder and cannibalism by a madman convinced that all humans must die in order to preserve the natural world for himself.

This mysterious killer, armed to the teeth for his 'war against humanity,' forces Derrick to follow in his bloody footsteps across Argentina. But with each life he takes, Derrick finds it harder to drop the weapon in his hand.

GARVEY'S EATS - Kenneth Seward

Deep in the backwoods of Texas sits a diner named Garvy's Eats, famous for its burger, the Garvy Special. Whitney and Tegan, best friends since Jr. High, are on a road trip to Mexico before college starts in the fall. After a thunderstorm forces the friends to take a detour, they end up at the diner where Roy Garvy wants the two girls for meat on the Garvy Special. Now with a monstrous, sick and twisted man known only as the Hellbilly hunting them down, the two girls must fight for their lives or risk ending up being served on a bun with a side of fries.

**A HellBound Books LLC
Publication**

www.hellboundbookspublishing.com

Printed in the United States of America

Made in the USA
Middletown, DE
18 November 2023